Becker the Researcher

Other books by Andrew A. Marino

Electromagnetism & Life (with Robert O. Becker)
Electric Wilderness (with Joel Ray)
Going Somewhere: Truth About a Life in Science
Modern Bioelectricity

Further publications available at *andrewamarino.com*

BECKER THE RESEARCHER

Andrew A. Marino

CASSANDRA PUBLISHING, BELCHER, LA

Published by Cassandra Publishing
304 Caddo Street
Belcher, LA 71004

©2017 by Andrew A. Marino

For information: cassandra@cassandrapublishing.net

ISBN: 978-0-9818549-3-9

Library of Congress Control Number: 2017911547

To

Linda

Wife, and partner

For life

Contents

———————————

Prologue

As I approached the end of a long and satisfying career in science, I felt the necessity to tell the story of Dr. Robert Becker, whom I consider to have been one of the most interesting, altruistic, and important although generally unknown men of science and medicine from the last century. I gained an understanding of him during the sixteen years I worked in his laboratory. When it closed in 1979, ending his odyssey in research and my time with him, I had the impression he was a great man who had an unyielding nature. Inflamed by what I had learned from him, I started my own laboratory and for many years did experiments that followed the path he had charted. Events that occurred during that period helped me evaluate his achievements in the context of time, which facilitated distinguishing between the worthwhile and the insignificant. Following his death in 2008 I decided that my experience and level of maturity were sufficient to guide my selection of stories to tell so that you might more readily understand his character and accomplishments. I offer this book, far from perfect as it is, in the hope of conveying a sense of the heights of thinking he reached, the level of abstraction he achieved, how deeply he saw into the nature of medicine, and the single-minded determination with which he pursued his goals. The story is about who he was, what he sought, why, and the consequences he faced, which I am leaving so that he will be remembered with the admiration he deserves.

The passage of so many years has not dulled my recollections of him, which were aided by the laboratory records he left me, his letters to me after we parted, and the many remembrances I have of him, the most treasured of which surround me now as I write—his pen-and-ink drawings of Galvani's experiments; an electrical model of bone's response to injury constructed by painstakingly soldering an interlaced network of numerous resistors; a photograph of him operating his prized spectrometer; an oil painting he made of the rural environment of upstate New York that he loved so much; his watercolor of an old red barn; a photo taken the day he received the Middleton Award; and the newspaper headline that appeared the day his laboratory closed, "International Authority on Regeneration Quits."

His physical features and mannerisms impressed me strongly from the beginning, and never ceased to impress me. He was of average height but so slim that he seemed taller. During our conversations his eyes would remain firmly fixed on mine when he spoke, their intensity seemingly magnified by the glasses he wore. The firmness of his jaw was accentuated when he was smoking a pipe, which he did frequently. He had a long face that extended from the tip of his jutting jaw to the top of his head, where his hairline began. His countenance gave the impression of a determined man on a serious mission. His personality, the spell of his words, and the sharpness of his mind have always remained vivid to me.

When I began working in his laboratory, the edifice of science appeared to me to be like a great book of Truth, the Word of God written in atoms and energy for the edification of the chosen few. Now I can see that the book contains something far less certain than I had imagined, more shadowy, fragmented, and always incomplete. I learned things about the ways of the world and ultimately came to an understanding of how a valiant and highly ethical man who generated unique insights into the scientific basis of the human condition, who constructed a general plan to find truths that mattered, and who obtained the resources needed to accomplish this task, could ultimately fall victim to a common folly manifested by many great men in literature and in life. So I have written about him, and connected my observations and impressions with what I learned from talking to witnesses whom I thought trustworthy. Occasionally, to make the events I relate more comprehensible, I will describe what the world of science and medicine was like and what was happening, as I understood these things then and remember them now in the light of what I learned, doing the best I can to identify and interrelate the important developments, some of which were confusing.

Chapter 1.

Physician

1923–1956: He grows up in New York, attends medical school, serves in the army, becomes an orthopedic surgeon, and chooses a career in biomedical research

Robert Becker was born in 1923, the only child of a Lutheran minister and his wife, both German. He grew up in Long Island, New York, graduated in 1945 from a Lutheran College, by which time he had already served two years in the Army, and married Lillian Moller in 1946. After finishing medical school at New York University in 1948, he interned for a year at Bellevue Hospital and for the next seven years studied pathology, surgery, and orthopedic surgery, and served as a medical officer in the Army. His training in orthopedics, the clinical area in which he chose to specialize, took place mostly at the Veterans Administration hospital in Brooklyn.

According to him, orthopedic surgery at that time typically attracted athletes or lower-ranking medical students. Before I began writing this book, I had never thought about the reason he chose that specialty. He did not engage in sports when I knew him, except for fishing if that counts. He liked to take long walks in the country, which required stamina, particularly in the winter, but that is not the kind of athletic ability I think he had in mind when he described the prototypical orthopedist. In medical school he had been elected to Alpha Omega Alpha, so he was probably competitive for any specialty that appealed to him. Perhaps during his youth he had an inspirational encounter with an orthopedist, which is a common reason given by orthopedic residency applicants when they are forced to explain why they chose orthopedics. There may have been a deeper reason. I wish I had asked him.

From how he talked about his background, I saw that even as a young medical student he had begun to chafe at the role dogma played in medical practice. One day in his first clinical year, a diagnostic issue concerning a patient arose during rounds. In the presence of other students and staff, all standing and listening around the patient's bed, Dr. Becker offered his assessment of the patient but was humiliated by his professor who rejected

Dr. Becker's reasoning not because it was inconsistent with the clinical facts but purely as an authoritarian act of dominance. That experience, and likely others that had similar psychological impacts, left their stamps on his character.

He told many stories that, looking back now and understanding him better as I do, I can see were really about his developing sense of dissatisfaction concerning how physicians were taught to think. Once while looking through a microscope at thin sections of human tissue that had been stained with dyes to enhance various features, he realized that his attention was focused on the appearance of the tissue rather than on thinking about how it had functioned before it died. He had come to see that making meaning from what he called "painted tombstones" was like trying to diagnose a wanderer from footprints left behind. The distinction between structure and function always remained important to him, and he often characterized the failure to appreciate it as emblematic of a trend in clinical medicine toward becoming too objectified and technologically oriented, treating patients not as human beings but as if they actually were their test results and x-rays.

Another story that hinted at the early development of his perspective regarding medicine occurred when he was a ward officer treating soldiers who had fractured bones. He began to think seriously about the healing process and wondered how the body knew that a fracture had occurred, what initiated the healing response, how it was controlled, and what ended it after healing was complete. These questions were largely unstudied even though the final result was something amazing, the growth of new bone that was indistinguishable from uninjured bone. The exact replacement of what was lost. True regeneration. "How does that happen," he said to me, "and with such consistency that we are surprised when the bone doesn't heal?" Another time he put the issue this way, "How does the body know to grow arm bone in the arm and leg bone in the leg, and not the other way around?" He felt alone in these thoughts, as if there was no one else who shared them, at least not among those with whom he worked, or the authors of the textbooks he was studying. And some things that were in the books did not ring true for him, like the notion that healing was a thing done by the physician using medicine or surgery, rather than something done by the patient based on intrinsic capabilities. His attitude on this point was fully formed and vital in his philosophy by the time I had first met him, and never changed throughout his lifetime.

By the end of his medical studies he had developed a sense that the medical profession did not encompass some sound and potentially beneficial perspectives, like a house that was too small. Despite the limited extent of his scientific training and medical experience, probably sometime in 1955 he decided to devote his life to clinically relevant research aimed at addressing what he saw as shortcomings regarding the medical wisdom he had received. Now and then he talked to me fondly about one of his professors, and he delighted in the few instances when he had an opportunity to show them the progress he had made. I never knew whether any of those professors had actually influenced his choice of a career in research. Perhaps the regard he expressed was just the remembrance of a man looking back on his life and trying to create order and necessity out of past events. The only explanation I can offer for his life-shaping decision to devote his career to research is that it emerged by some mysterious process, based on a combination of his genes, medical training and experience, and the values he had been taught in his youth.

Knowing all I do about his life and his work, and nearing the end of my career in biomedical research that was guided by his perspective and motivated by his gospel from which I deviated only in some details, I still have only scant understanding of whether he believed he had a chance of being successful, or even of knowing what counted as success. He had never formally studied how to do research, and had no more training in science than the minimum needed to qualify as a licensed physician, a level of training well below that of the scientists who were then shaping the development of medicine. Nevertheless he boldly pursued his goal, I suppose in the expectation that methodological issues could be mastered as necessary.

He knew that a position at a Veterans Administration hospital would allow him to combine practicing medicine with clinically oriented research. For most physicians, working at a VA hospital was an unattractive career choice because of the low salary, prohibition on engaging in private practice, and the monotonous chronic medical problems that had to be treated. As an employment perk, the Veterans Administration had what amounted to a noncompetitive research program that allowed individual hospitals to award staff physicians the time, laboratory space, and funds to perform research, all of which were promised to him when he was offered a position as chief of orthopedics at the Syracuse VA hospital. In June 1956, the month he finished his residency, he accepted the offer and continued in that position until 1979 when he went into exile, never having worked anyplace else. There is perhaps no historical parallel in science or even in fiction for the nature, motivation, and circumstances of his decision to devote his professional life to research and then to successfully implement that decision in a career that reached great heights before it ended tragically.

Chapter 2.

Researcher

1956–1958: He begins practicing medicine, initiates research on muscle disorders, publishes his first paper, and becomes dissatisfied with his progress

During his first year at the VA hospital Dr. Becker organized the orthopedic service, established clinics, created operating-room procedures and on-call schedules, and began networking with the other specialists on the hospital staff. About the middle of his second year he was finally able to think about research, and he turned his attention toward identifying a suitable project. The ongoing research by the other staff physicians was of low quality and offered no potential beginning point for his work. Higher quality work was in progress in the medical school of the State University of New York in Syracuse, which was located on the same campus as the VA hospital. He had an unsalaried faculty appointment in the Department of Surgery, but the local culture did not encourage cooperative research projects between the VA staff and the full-time faculty at the medical school, even assuming that was what he wanted.

He became interested in a type of musculoskeletal problem that he encountered in his orthopedic clinic. The disorder presented as a severe muscle weakness in which the patients had difficulty walking and sometimes even moving their arms. The source of the problem, whether muscles, nerves, or the immune system, was unknown and there was no agreement among the medical specialists regarding what signs and symptoms were necessary before the disorder could be diagnosed as "polymyositis." Medical texts on microscopic examination of muscle biopsies described the presence of degenerated muscle fibers and inflammation in patients with muscle weakness, but the biopsy results from most of his symptomatic patients were normal. He suspected that the disorder stemmed from a failure of the nerves to properly control the muscles. Nerves were known to work by passing electrical impulses, but the information transmitted by that process lasted for only a fraction of a second. The impulse process was a good explanation for sensation and muscle activation, but could not explain phenomena that lasted more than a moment, like chronic muscle weakness. He believed there had to be unrecognized ways of transmitting the type of information that controlled long-lasting phenomena. He got the idea that nerves continuously transmitted information by a process that did not involve the impulses.

Nationally only a few investigators directly studied nerves because specialized training and access to experimental animals were required. But electrical signals in muscles could readily be measured in patients, and that was what he decided to do. The local research committee approved his plan and authorized funds for an instrument that recorded and displayed the signals, and a motion-picture camera that photographed them as they appeared on the screen of the instrument. In symptomatic patients, he inserted needle electrodes into the muscles that were weak and those that were not, and compared the signals as the patients moved their limbs. The signals consisted of a series of numerous rapid spikes, and he looked for unusual patterns from the weak muscles that could warrant a diagnosis of polymyositis. Eventually he found the patterns he was looking for, or at least he believed he did. Based on a report that rats fed a diet deficient in vitamin E had developed weak muscles, he treated his patients with vitamin E and found that the signals from weak muscles became normalized and the patients' symptoms improved.

His research ambitions expanded after he contacted Ragnar Granit, an expert in nerves and muscles who was working at the Rockefeller Institute. Granit was interested in the possibility that so-called gamma nerve cells might mediate some forms of muscle behavior, and had already found gamma cells in cats. Dr. Becker asked him what type of muscle signal he would expect if humans also had gamma nerve cells. In the course of their correspondence Granit suggested that Dr. Becker measure muscle signals produced by passive motion of the patient's limb, rather than by relying on the patient to move it. When he attempted to do so he encountered serious problems obtaining and interpreting the data. Even when he repeated a measurement many times, near the limit of how often a patient could tolerate repositioning the needles, signals from the same muscle often differed markedly, which confused the tasks of comparing signals from different muscles. But he persisted, and he told me that was when he first began to understand how to extract meaning from his data.

Basic scientists are taught to repeat a measurement many times and regard the average as true knowledge, even though the average typically differs from almost all of the individual measurements. Physicians learn a different method for obtaining knowledge. They are routinely presented with a broad range of observable signs, symptoms, and historical facts pertaining to a patient and are required to make a diagnosis and plan a course of treatment on the basis of only the relevant information, which is always a minuscule fraction of the available information. Physicians are taught that knowledge of what information is relevant comes from the physician's training, experience, and degree of intuitive insight. Dr. Becker found that obvious differences in the signals from different muscles disappeared when he averaged the measurements, indicating that the method of averaging was inapplicable to evaluation of the muscle signals because it failed to capture the reality, like the man with his head in an oven and his feet in a refrigerator whose body temperature was normal, on average. He instinctively viewed the part of science that applied to medicine as properly approachable using the method of the physician, and in doing so went beyond the method for producing knowledge that he had learned in his classes on basic science.

One of the problems he faced involved deciding whether an individual measurement was reliable. If too much movement occurred when he inserted the needle, or if it went too deep or not deep enough into the muscle, or entered a blood vessel, then even in principle the recorded signal could not reflect what he intended to measure. No textbook or meter can tell an experimentalist how to decide whether a particular meter reading actually reflects the physiological process under study or is an artifact caused by uncontrolled changes in the conditions of the measurement. On the other hand, the reading may simply be inconsistent with the study hypothesis rather than artifactual. Such measurements are unwanted but valid and must be accepted, so you can see that the reliability of scientific knowledge is absolutely dependent on objective ethical decision-making by investigators. They must record what they see not what they desire, and they must be honest enough to accept the difference.

Dr. Becker also confronted the experimentalist's most difficult problem, making meaning from the measurements. Every measurement is only a sign of a sign, and the experimentalist's task is to identify the deeper sign to which the measurements point. "The data speaks for itself" is often said, but no one who understands biomedical research would ever agree with that ugly proposition. The meaning of the shifting patterns he saw on the display screen of his recording device came from his mind, after due consideration of their actual structure, the conditions under which they were recorded, and the history of similar measurements.

He submitted a report on his observations and conclusions about the meaning of the signals for publication in the *Journal of Bone and Joint Surgery*, the most prestigious journal in his specialty, and received many criticisms from the anonymous reviewers. Some argued that the measured signals were artifacts due to motion of the electrodes. Others said the signals came from nerves, not muscles, or disputed whether there was enough evidence to show that the signals changed in a predictable way during successive passive movements of the limb. Objections were raised to the absence of data averaging and to the use of the narrative form in which Results were not brightly separated from the Discussion. In his eyes almost all the objections were intended to tear down his work because it presented evidence that seemed to go against orthodoxy, not because there were actual shortcomings in the work. The anonymity of the reviewers allowed them to take liberties in tone and syntax that would have been regarded as highly offensive had they been delivered face-to-face. The reviewers forced him to make changes he bitterly opposed; otherwise they threatened to recommend rejection of the paper. He regarded the final version as incoherent and never referred to it after publication even though the existence of gamma cells in humans ultimately became universally recognized. Even years later, when he told me the details, he still roiled with anger.

Although bloodied, he remained unbowed, and the meteoric phase of his career began. He entered a world whose artificial limitations on scientific knowledge about human beings he saw more clearly than anyone else in his time.

Chapter 3.

Headway

1958–1959: He finds slowly varying voltages in patients, relates them to growth control, and plans new experiments

During the muscle studies Dr. Becker noticed that when he touched two needles to the patient's skin without penetrating it, the trace on the screen of the recording instrument was a flat line with no spikes or waves. If he held the needles in place for a while, the vertical position of the trace changed indolently, indicating that he was observing a slowly varying DC voltage emanating from the patient. The voltages, which unquestionably were not produced by muscles, appeared between any two points on the body and he guessed that they did not originate in the skin but deeper in the body, probably in nerves, and somehow propagated to the skin like non-DC voltages such as those produced by the heart and the brain. Nothing he had learned during his medical studies ever suggested that DC voltages could be measured on human skin. The only relevant work he found in the literature was that of Harold Burr, a professor of anatomy at Yale University.

Beginning in 1916, Burr had begun publishing research articles dealing with how a single cell in a salamander egg developed into a fully formed salamander. For years his work was prosaic but in 1932, like Athena emerging from Zeus's brow, he suddenly proposed a stunningly speculative theory regarding how the development occurred. His data consisted only of rates of cell division and qualitative observations of the growth pattern of nerves as assessed from microscope slides of embryonic tissue. The rates increased dramatically at the same time that the nerves appeared in the region of the dividing cells. In what he called a "somewhat theoretical discussion of the facts," he reasoned there must have been a physical law that initiated and regulated the rate of cell division and a physical law that governed the appearance of the nerves in the region, and he wondered how the two processes were coordinated so that they always occurred together. One possibility was that the dividing cells secreted an unknown substance and the nerves naturally grew toward its source. Another possibility was that the nerves could have released a biochemical that had the power to trigger cell division. The evidence in favor of either possibility was nil but both fit within the biochemical theory of biology, the orthodox framework for explaining life processes. As an alternative to the orthodoxy, and not presaged by anything he had written previously, he hypothesized that electromagnetic energy existed naturally at every point inside the embryo and controlled its growth, so that the successive developmental stages followed each other in regular order. Each stage was guided by, contributed to, and modified the flow of the electromagnetic energy, which he regarded as the unifying principle responsible for integrating myriad local biochemical processes to produce regulated growth and development that resulted in new animals that always looked more or less as expected.

Under his hypothesis that electromagnetic energy existed everywhere in the developing embryo, a DC voltage should be present between any two locations in the embryo, and also between any two points in the salamander after it hatched. No one had ever measured omnipresent DC voltages of the type that he supposed existed. Anyone who might have attempted to do so would likely have used metal electrodes, which were suitable for rapidly changing signals like those from muscles, brain, or heart but were inherently incapable of reliably measuring DC voltages in tissue. Moreover, even if the DC voltages were present and could be measured, they would be extraordinarily weak, perhaps able to guide cellular activity as he theorized but certainly not strong enough to produce a DC current that could activate the kind of meters for measuring voltages that were then available. Burr recognized both problems and solved them. He essentially invented the use of nonmetallic electrodes for DC voltage measurements from animal tissues, and he built a voltmeter that could detect the characteristically weak voltages they produce, an advance made possible by the recent invention of the vacuum tube. He then used the solutions to show that indolent DC voltages existed in the embryos, as he had predicted. He next discovered that DC voltages also occurred between any two points on the skin of the animals after they hatched, which led him to speculate that the voltages might also be responsible for guiding postnatal growth. If so, he reasoned, then pharmacologic or surgical interventions known to affect growth should affect the voltages, and he repeatedly proved that this indeed was the case. In study after study published in famous journals during the thirties, forties, and fifties, he showed that the DC voltages were somehow connected with life processes, not only in salamanders but also in the entire range of multicellular organisms from slime molds to humans. He published his ninety-third and last experimental study the same year Dr. Becker began working at the VA hospital.

Burr's publications had lain undisturbed as if in a coffin until Dr. Becker discovered them in the basement of the medical school library. He realized that the work resonated with his deeply held wonder at how the body somehow knew when and where it had been injured, and exactly how to execute an effective healing response. When Burr and Dr. Becker looked at a living organism, respectively from the perspectives of a developmental biologist and a physician, they both saw systemic emergent phenomena as critically important but fundamentally unexplained. One day Dr. Becker got the idea that the DC voltages he had measured might be the key part of the grand system by which the body healed itself. He conceptualized the voltages as part of a physiological command and control system that transmitted information-bearing natural electromagnetic energy via nerves from the brain, where a control plan resided, like data in a computer, to locations in the body where a specific kind of healing was needed. In that manner, he speculated, the system ultimately determined health and disease.

***

So that you can better appreciate the obstacles Dr. Becker faced and the loneliness he must have felt as he pressed forward with his research, I will interrupt my story to tell you what the world of science was like at that time, and how it got to be that way.

In physics, the straightforward idea of matter and the more abstract idea of energy developed and became the foundation for a small set of universal laws that governed all phenomena manifested by inanimate matter. The laws were of the type that allowed the phenomena they controlled to be conceptually divided into parts whose dynamical activities could be analyzed experimentally in isolation from those of the other parts. The individual analyses could then be added together to explain the phenomena. Called "reductionism," the method of explaining phenomena by combining explanations of their parts was highly successful and its fruit was technology.

Human biology developed differently. The rational philosopher René Descartes defined a human being as a machine operated by a soul. The machine metaphor became permanent, but the notion of a soul was rejected by scientists even though they had no better explanation for the process that made the machine move. Then, during the first half of the twentieth century, men interested in learning how biochemical reactions created life, the Fathers of experimental biology, motivated by profound respect for the achievements of the physicists, adopted their cognitive structure as the canonical basis for explaining the phenomena manifested by living systems. In this manner mathematical law became recognized as the ghost that moved the machine, Descartes' soul, and reductionism was adopted as the exclusive methodological basis of experimental biology, as was the case in physics.

The Fathers believed that reductionism would ultimately lead to discovery of the laws that governed living systems, but they had no knowledge of mathematics, the sublime language of physics, and consequently had no inkling of the ineluctable implications of their decision to ape the thought system of physics. As it happened, the laws that governed inanimate matter were relatively simple in the mathematical sense and therefore amenable to discovery using reductionism. But the laws that governed system-level biological phenomena like growth, healing, memory, consciousness, health, or the occurrence of any of the chronic diseases exhibit a type of complexity that renders them insusceptible of discovery using only reductionism. So you can see that the biological canon adopted by the Fathers eliminated the possibility of achieving a deep understanding of precisely the aspects of life that people care about the most.

I would like to be able to say that I have already described the breadth of the historical errors of the Fathers, but I haven't yet described their most serious error. Almost without exception they were biochemists, and unsurprisingly they emphasized the importance of the role of chemical energy in explaining the phenomena exhibited by living systems. But they went too far and blessed chemical energy as the sole energy of life, thereby rejecting the possibility of a substantial role for the other forms of energy that had been found essential for explaining even the comparatively simple machines that give rise to the phenomena exhibited by inanimate matter. The most serious consequence of this extreme perspective was that the laws of electromagnetic energy largely disappeared from experimental biology.

Having made their choices, the Fathers strongly defended them from their bully pulpits as heads of grant-awarding committees, journal editors, and textbook authors. The result was that the conception of life as a simple chemical machine amenable to understanding by means of reductionism became entrenched. The heirs of the Fathers learned how to explain the beating heart, the flow of blood, the formation of the nerve impulse, the contraction of muscle, the conversion of food into chemical energy, the operation of genes, and how proteins are made, all processes governed by relatively simple laws. But the heirs were inherently incapable of rationalizing any claim of knowledge regarding system-level phenomena because their cognitive structure did not recognize a method by which the governing laws could be discovered, and it is axiomatic in science that scientific knowledge is the product of method. Thus although the experimental biology the Fathers handed down answered some important questions, it did not answer or even legalize study of phenomena that emerge only at or above the level of the cell, including life itself. Instead such questions became regarded as nonscientific, suitable only for philosophers.

Researchers who came after the Fathers survived only if they ignored system-level biology and concentrated on the parts of a cell, and the parts of their parts, spiraling ever downward in focus and objective. The ironic result was that the heirs of the Fathers ceased studying life and concentrated on molecules, a level of reality at which the concept of life has no meaning. Recognition of roles for system biology, nonchemical energy, and nonreductionist experimental strategies in explaining life, health, or disease are nowhere to be found in their textbooks.

System biology was exactly what interested Burr, particularly the unrecognized problem of how the biochemical reactions that produce growth which occur simultaneously throughout the body were coordinated, something he recognized that chemical energy couldn't explain because it always acted locally rather than at a distance. His proposed answer was a system-wide flow of electromagnetic energy. But neither the question nor the answer had any perceived merit in the eyes of the Fathers, who saw it as an attempt to resurrect the long-discredited Cartesian concept that human beings were animated by a soul. Burr's studies remained buried until Dr. Becker discovered them.

***

While focusing on the modern work involving nerves that could possibly serve as a rationale for connecting them with DC voltages and healing, Dr. Becker came upon an article by Marcus Singer in *Scientific American* that dealt with regeneration of body parts. Singer had posed the question of why adult salamanders can regrow amputated limbs but frogs and all other evolutionarily more advanced animals cannot regenerate limbs or any body parts. Based on experiments he concluded that the key factor was the amount of nerve tissue in the limb, that frogs and all other more advanced animals did not have enough nerve tissue in their extremities to permit limb regeneration. Dr. Becker told me that his general thinking at the point in his career I am now describing was also affected by the theory of Thomas Hunt Morgan that higher animals couldn't regenerate limbs because they apparently lacked an electrical control system that could synchronize the chemical signals that appeared following an injury. Sometime in mid-1958 the threads of Morgan, Singer, and Burr somehow came together for Dr. Becker and he identified system-wide slowly varying DC voltages generated and transmitted by the nervous system as fundamentally important in controlling growth and healing processes in adult animals.

He was keenly aware that attempting to explain growth control would be seen by mainstream experimental biologists as trying to explain life, akin to moving from science into philosophy or religion. In their perspective, growth and life were simply conditions of the world, like gravity, not something to be explained, mechanistically or otherwise. The only person he knew of who had attempted to explain life was Albert Szent-Gyorgyi, and he had not fared well. Dr. Becker realized he had to construct a plausible narrative for the DC voltages that explained why they deserved consideration. A timely article in *Science* materially aided the development of his story. The author, Harold Bullock, described how a recently discovered inter-cell structure called a "gap junction" allowed electromagnetic energy to flow between nerve cells. Dr. Becker recognized that the discovery had the effect of converting the cells into a long-distance transmission line that could operate in a way which was unrelated to the recognized nerve-impulse mechanism, and he incorporated this element into his story.

During this formative period of his research career the Soviet Union began launching Sputniks. One of the U.S. government's responses was to begin translating Soviet scientific journals and making the information broadly available in the United States. Bundles of articles from different Soviet journals were assembled into reports and sent to various federal installations, one of which was the Syracuse VA hospital library. The reports were unorganized and the quality of the translations was poor, which prevented systematic study of any particular topic. Nevertheless when Dr.

Becker scanned the translations he came across many instances involving plants, animals, and humans where DC voltages had been studied and where man-made DC currents had been applied. He saw that bioelectrical science existed in the Soviet Union, quite unlike the situation in the U.S., and he took this fact as a kind of validation of his ideas.

Experimentation in biology, it seemed to him, was an endless process of division into smaller and smaller pieces that discounted to near zero the relationships between the pieces and elevated to near maximum the importance of their individuality. He believed strongly that the system perspective was also valid, and that was the direction he headed. The experimental biologists who had preceded him were motivated principally by the sheer desire to know, and to do something they enjoyed. Dr. Becker also loved knowledge, but his work had an ethical dimension not present in the work of most others, a deeply felt responsibility to do experiments whose results had a reasonable possibility of ultimately helping patients. He had the eye of an artist, the ambition of a scientist seeking natural explanations for natural phenomena, an indomitable spirit, and a desire to act in the way he thought best regardless of the opinions of those who disagreed with him.

Rene Descartes

Harold Burr

Chapter 4.

Discovery

1960–1961: He identifies the source of the DC voltages, discovers their relationship to limb regeneration, shows they produce detectable currents in nerves, describes their connection with normal human cycles and mental disorders, and infers they form a link between man and the environment

According to Dr. Becker, information that controlled growth and healing was contained in electromagnetic energy that was continuously transmitted by nerves, a process which produced the DC voltages. In his journal notes on Burr's studies he wrote, "Still have not found paper with locations of the DC voltages. I wonder if it has been published!" It hadn't, so that was where he decided to begin, expecting that the spatial pattern of the voltages on the skin of salamanders would reflect the anatomical organization of the salamander's nervous system.

He asked the local research committee for funds to buy salamanders and other supplies needed to make the measurements. The heads of the physiology and biochemistry departments told him that his proposal was not properly conceived because it was not biochemically based. Robert Chodos, the committee chairman and head of the research service at the hospital, told Dr. Becker that studying electrical signals in animals would be a waste of VA funds. After he reminded Chodos of the VA's promise of research support, the committee agreed to leave the funding decision to the local expert on the biology of salamanders, an anatomy professor named Chester Yntema. He too warned against making electrical measurements, but his attitude toward Dr. Becker was like that of a father toward his son. I was not privy to the details of their discussions but I learned the gist of what Yntema said. If the voltages existed, he told Dr. Becker, they had no important role. And even if they were important, proving it would be impossible because the results of any experiment would have many different interpretations, but none that could compel general acceptance. Nevertheless he gave his approval and counseled Dr. Becker to follow his own lights, saying, "You have the right to fail."

Using electrodes of the type Burr had designed and commercial versions of the voltmeter he had developed, Dr. Becker systematically measured the DC voltages that appeared on the skin of anesthetized adult salamanders. The depth of the anesthesia affected the voltage values, which was his first indication of a fundamental connection between the nervous system and the DC voltages. He adjusted the anesthetic dose for each animal so that it lost consciousness only long enough to permit him to make the measurements. Touching the electrodes to the animal's skin affected the readings because of small unavoidable changes in the contact pressure between the electrode tip and the animal's skin. He eliminated the artifact by using salt-saturated nylon wicks, which exerted no pressure at the contact point.

He measured the DC voltage at predetermined locations on the skin of a series of salamanders. Random factors sometimes affected the reliability of a particular measurement, so determining whether the overall results correlated with the anatomy of the nervous system depended heavily on recognizing and eliminating the bad measurements. And even when a measurement was reliable, not every animal exhibited exactly the same voltage at a given anatomical location. Nevertheless the pattern of values in individual animals consistently correlated with the anatomy of the nervous system, as he had predicted. He reported the results in the top U.S. biomedical engineering journal, using data from representative animals rather than from some mythical average animal that didn't exist, which was how the results likely would have been reported by an investigator who was less attuned to the nature of the signal he was measuring, and to the reason he was measuring it. So Dr. Becker was able to demonstrate what Burr's work had portended, that there was a relationship between the DC voltages and the organization of the nervous system.

He envisioned the DC voltages as somehow originating in nerves and forming the working part of a control system that shuffled information around the body by means of a flow of electromagnetic energy. This putative communication system was centered in the brain where the control principles, what today would be called "algorithms," were located and connected by an energy flow to regional processes that mediated growth, the prototypes of which for him were the automatic healing of a bone fracture in humans and the ability of salamanders to regenerate an entire limb. This focus on particular healing phenomena permitted him to employ experimental manipulations in a way that none of his predecessors had done. He developed specific testable hypotheses, an approach he described as, "If I'm right, then if I do this I should observe that."

His first test was to cut the spinal cord at the level of the brain stem and when he did the voltages on the skin disappeared, consistent with his theory. Leaving the spinal cord intact but sectioning the nerves at the point they exited from the cord and passed into the limbs caused the voltages on the skin of the limbs to drop to near zero within a few seconds, again exactly as expected. Next he tested the theory even more dramatically. Knowing that salamanders and frogs reacted to loss of a limb in quite different ways, he amputated one hind limb in animals of both species and measured the injury-site DC voltage that occurred daily after amputation. In both species, amputation was followed immediately by a rapid shift from negative to positive in the polarity of the injury-site voltage. But the daily changes in the voltages during healing differed greatly between the two species. In frogs, the voltage decreased slowly toward the negative value that had existed at the end of the limb prior to amputation. The accompanying healing response consisted only of the growth of skin over the stump. The temporal pattern of voltage in salamanders was quite different. The voltage at the amputation site decreased from the positive value that had occurred immediately after amputation to a highly negative value, and then slowly increased toward its normal, more moderately negative value. The growth of new limbs accompanied the voltage change. In his mind the results of the study were pregnant with the notion that the inter-species difference in healing was somehow related to the difference in the time course of the post-amputation DC voltages.

Fracture healing is a regenerative phenomenon exhibited by both species. His theory of a relationship between the pattern of DC voltage changes following injury and whether regeneration occurred predicted that the two species should show a similar temporal pattern following fracture. And further, according to the theory, the pattern should resemble the pattern exhibited by salamanders during limb regeneration. He was unable to perform the experiment in salamanders because their limbs were too small to reliably reproduce an experimental fracture, an absolute requirement for a valid study. He was able to perform the experiment in frogs, and as he hypothesized, the DC voltages following a fracture changed with time in a manner similar to the changes shown by salamanders during limb regeneration.

He interpreted his observations as evidence that the DC activity in the nervous system was an integral part of a data transmission and control system that regulated regeneration and repair. He speculated that a change in the electromagnetic energy transmitted by nerves occurred as a consequence of injury, and that the change triggered accumulation of cell types capable of organizing into a new limb. In this fashion, brain-sourced electromagnetic energy was linked to cells in the limbs in a closed loop that fed information back to the brain during the healing process, thereby progressively blunting the effect of the initial stimulus produced by the injury, a relationship he termed "negative feedback." The report of the study appeared in the *Journal of Bone and Joint Surgery*.

Some investigators at the medical school encouraged Dr. Becker to move his experiments in the direction of trying to understand the biochemistry of the growth-control system, and he received offers of access to laboratories where biochemical studies could be carried out. He resolutely declined all such offers, choosing instead to maintain an intense focus on demonstrating the existence of medically significant phenomena rather than allowing himself to become sidetracked doing mechanistic studies, which he regarded as proper work for PhD's, investigators who pursue biochemical minutiae for personal edification in contrast to MD's who study the whole organism for the benefit of patients. Thus he continued on his treacherous journey alone, like someone who goes to sea in a small boat.

The melancholy and frustration he had experienced during his first years at the VA were washed away by the exciting progress of his research, and the satisfaction he found in his clinical work. He gave the hospital employees medical advice whenever they asked, which made him a favorite, someone they would help in any way they could. When the elevator operators sensed he was in a hurry they would skip floors to get him to his floor more quickly. No other staff physician was as approachable by the ordinary workers at the hospital as was Dr. Becker, but his relationship with the hospital administrators was stiff; he had a low opinion of their collective competence which was reflected in his interactions with them, at least that is what I was told.

When he planned his next experiment he assumed that the presence of a DC voltage between the head and the extremities of the salamander meant that an actual DC current was flowing between them, as if they were connected by a wire. The existence of a current in a wire could be confirmed by cutting it and attaching an ammeter between the cut ends. That option did not exist for him, however, because a nerve was not a homogeneous structure like a wire but rather consisted of thousands of exceedingly long cells, each of which would have been injured by transecting the nerve, with no hope of connecting them to a meter to measure the pre-injury current. He contacted Charles Bachman, a physics professor at Syracuse University and the man who would later become the head of my dissertation committee when I received my PhD, and asked how the currents he supposed were flowing in the nerves could be measured. Initially, Bachman suggested the possibility that the voltages might be better explained without assuming the existence of an actual flow of current over long distances because only a flow of electromagnetic energy was needed to sustain his theory. The example he offered was that of an ordinary battery sitting on a shelf—it had a voltage but not a current. But Dr. Becker's belief that the DC voltages were caused by currents had taken strong root, and Bachman later told me he thought he had no good reason to challenge Dr. Becker in matters involving physiology.

From Bachman, Dr. Becker learned about the "Hall effect," a standard method for detecting the existence of a current flow in ordinary electrical conductors. He acquired a strong permanent magnet, a necessary tool for detecting the Hall effect, and began performing Hall studies on live salamanders, seeking to detect the actual "effect," a tiny signal whose existence would evidence a current flow.

A Hall measurement is not a simple matter and had never previously been attempted in a living animal. Nevertheless he persisted and ultimately observed the signal he expected, which he took to mean that there was indeed a real current that naturally passed from the spinal cord into the extremities. The editors of *Science*, one of the world's premier scientific journals, accepted his results, agreed with his interpretation, and published his report of the study. I will have more to say about it later.

If the DC voltages were a result of the flow of current in the nerves as he supposed, he was faced with the problem of explaining why the current always seemed to go in one direction, outward from the brain and through the spinal cord into the limbs, as if the current were piling up at the end of its journey, or simply disappearing. His solution furnished another example of his ability to see what underlies the complexity of living things, like an artist who captures a scene before rendering it on canvas. By means of electrical impulses, nerves carry sensory information to the brain and send brain-generated information to muscles. At the level of an individual nerve cell, impulses were known to always move in only one direction, from the end of the cell where they begin to the other end where they trigger the release of biochemicals that initiate formation of impulses in the next cell in the pathway. He reasoned that the DC current carried by nerves moved in the same fashion, out from the brain along the motor nerves to muscles, and back again via the sensory nerves from the places in the body where the impulses that code for sensation begin. This stunning association of the currents with the known anatomical organization of the nervous system ensured that the current ended in the same place it began, which is a fundamental characteristic of any electrical circuit.

He tested the idea of oppositely flowing currents in motor and sensory nerves by measuring the change in the DC voltages that occurred point by point along sciatic nerves in frogs. When he made measurements in an exposed but intact sciatic nerve, the end of the nerve farthest from the spinal cord was always negative, as he had observed earlier when he made the measurements on the skin above the nerve. But the sciatic nerve branches into two distinct nerves in the region of the thigh, one that carries mostly sensory signals up to the brain and one that carries mostly motor signals down to the muscles. As he had hypothesized, the polarities of the voltages in the branches were opposite, plus to minus in one and minus to plus in the other, indicating, according to his conception, that the current responsible for the voltages was flowing in opposite directions in the two branches. The strengths of the two currents were not identical, and consequently an overall plus-to-minus voltage occurred in the sciatic nerve, which was the parent of the two branches. Those results were published in *Nature*, an even more famous journal than *Science*.

There were no experimental biologists who were doing experiments of the type he did, so his surprising observations had raised many questions that needed to be addressed before the theoretical structure he was erecting could begin to gain widespread support. But he seemed not to recognize a need to address the questions. His attitude was that he had explained what he did and what he observed, and that the implications were obvious. If someone believed that what he reported hadn't actually occurred under the circumstances described, then the critic should simply repeat the experiment and report the results. If someone believed that the data had been misinterpreted, then the critic should give his reasons and offer a more cogent interpretation. He had overcome these objections when journal reviewers raised them and he saw no reason to repeat himself. He proceeded to design experiments according to his own lights, without the benefit of dialogue with those who would argue with him, criticize his ideas, suggest clarifications, offer alternative explanations, or craft narratives that might be more acceptable to the "establishment," his term for the patrimony of the Fathers of experimental biology whose cognitive structure his work seemed to challenge. He didn't recognize that interactions with investigators who think differently from him were crucial for his development, as for any experimentalist.

He began making measurements of DC voltages on the skin of human subjects, intending to show that the voltages reflected the anatomy of the human nervous system, as in salamanders, but soon realized that the difference in size between salamanders and human beings meant that a huge number of measurements would be needed to confirm that the overall DC pattern reflected the organization of the human nervous system. He chanced to tell Howard Friedman, the chief of clinical psychology at the VA hospital, about voltage measurements in the head area and mentioned that the values appeared to depend on the attention level of the subjects. Friedman's own experiments at that time were aimed at developing objective measures of mental behavior, and he became interested in the possibility that the DC voltages might furnish the basis for detecting and quantifying the degree of severity of mental disorders. Working together, they measured DC voltages between the front and the back of the head in human volunteers and found that the front became more positive during sleep, anesthesia, and hypnosis, results that they reported in the *Archives of General Psychiatry*. The work pleased Dr. Becker, who saw it as a confirmation of similar results he had seen in anesthetized animals.

With a temerity that even now, a half century later, seems almost unbelievable to me, he boldly expanded the conceptual structure of his work. He reasoned that because artificial magnetic fields could affect the flow of electromagnetic energy in salamanders, as demonstrated in the Hall studies, the earth's magnetic field might also be able to cause a similar effect. The few people to whom he mentioned the idea told him it was an impossible concept because the magnetic field used in the Hall studies was a thousand times stronger than the earth's field, but he saw that argument as a non sequitur and doubled down on his supposition. Since the natural flow of electromagnetic energy was the basis of physiological regulation, he supposed further that any effect of the earth's field on the energy flow would have physiological consequences. Thinking in this manner he reached the momentous conclusion that the DC voltage system in the body was a link between living organisms and the environment.

While mulling over what experiments to do that could produce results supporting his far-reaching idea about the biological effects of magnetic fields, he came across recent reports in *Science* by two well-known biologists, Victor Twitty from Stanford and Frank Brown from Northwestern, whose scientific approaches were, like his, at the system level rather than biochemical level. Twitty had discovered a remarkable homing behavior exhibited by salamanders in which the adults returned to the same part of the stream where they had hatched, even from many miles away. Puzzled by how such a feat was possible, he had systematically considered various possibilities. In carefully done experiments he excluded explanations based on random searching or memorization of the landscape. Even animals that he had permanently blinded found their way back to where they had hatched, which eliminated any possible role for vision. Other experimental evidence indicated that neither hearing, smelling, nor tasting could explain the salamanders' migratory behavior. He could suggest no further plausible hypothesis, but Dr. Becker could. He got the idea that there must have been some factor in the environment that activated the salamander's sensory system. Whatever factor X was, it necessarily had certain specific characteristics. X had to have a unique value that was always present at each point on the earth, and the value had to be a vector because both magnitude and direction at each point were necessary to convey enough information to guide a purposeful migration. Moreover, X had to be such that trees, rocks, weather, or other animals did not distort it; X simply passed through them as if they weren't present. There was only one known physical entity that could satisfy these necessary criteria for serving as a signaling modality—the earth's magnetic field. He conceived the idea that the local magnetic field present at the time of the salamander's embryologic development was somehow imprinted on the animal's nervous system in such a fashion that subsequent mating and egg-laying activities would occur only at the location where the animal had hatched. A continuous flow of electromagnetic energy mediated an internal sensing system that detected the local magnetic field and presented position-dependent values to the brain which compared them with the stored values, a process that ultimately led the animal back to its birthplace.

Frank Brown had argued for many years with a biologist from Princeton named Colin Pittendrigh about what accounted for daily body rhythms, sleep for example. Pittendrigh was an ardent reductionist who argued that a biochemical clock in the brain governed biological rhythms. Brown was interested less in the mechanisms and more in the purpose of the rhythms, which he believed were evolutionarily conditioned. Under that hypothesis there had to be a factor X in the environment that could be detected by the body leading to a modification of the rhythm, and the X he chose for study was the earth's magnetic field. In laboratory studies that involved application of artificial earth-strength magnetic fields to worms and snails, he found that the animals behaved differently depending on the direction of the field he applied. According to Dr. Becker, the equipment Brown used didn't look "wissenschaftlich," consisting mainly of an inclined plane, a wooden board propped up at one end, with two cardboard boxes at the other end, only one of which contained a permanent magnet. Pittendrigh's laboratory, in contrast, contained an array of glass beakers, flasks, and tissue extractors, all connected by a complex network of glass tubing. But what Brown's set-up lacked in apparent sophistication it made up for in drama. In Pittendrigh's laboratory there were only bubbling liquids and bad smells, but in Brown's laboratory one saw snails move down the plane and turn either left or right, depending on which cardboard box contained the magnet, an experiment that a child could do but whose results could not be explained by the most erudite biologist.

In environmental studies, Brown found that the cyclic variation in cosmic rays striking the earth was correlated with the behavior of various primitive animals, particularly the fiddler crab. The reader should understand that changes in cosmic rays at the surface of the earth result from natural cyclic changes in the geomagnetic field, which affect its natural shielding of the earth's surface from cosmic rays. Brown believed that the changes in the cosmic rays were surrogates for what the crabs actually detected, the geomagnetic field.

What exactly happened at this point in time as regards Dr. Becker's interest in the idea that the body's electrical control system was susceptible to external magnetic influences will never be known because the three men involved in the pertinent events, Dr. Becker, Bachman, and Friedman, each told me versions that were inconsistent in pertinent details. I can only tell you what I think is the truest version of events.

Dr. Becker got the idea that humans, like Brown's crabs, might also exhibit behavioral changes that correlated with changes in the geomagnetic field. Bachman knew about the standard methods used by geophysicists to measure and record those changes, and about how to obtain that information from official government data repositories. Friedman suggested that admissions to psychiatric hospitals for schizophrenia might be a good behavioral endpoint for studying effects of geomagnetic changes. Such a study was possible then because psychotropic drugs hadn't been invented, so schizophrenics were institutionalized for treatment, and Friedman had access to the treatment records at the VA and Upstate hospitals. When he analyzed the records of schizophrenics who had been admitted during the previous four years, he found that when the geomagnetic field increased the number of hospital admissions also increased, a correlation that Dr. Becker had predicted.

Dr. Becker mentioned these provocative results when he presented his overall work at a meeting of the American Medical Association in June 1961. In the audience was an assistant director of the VA named Fred Panzer who worked in Central Office but had not previously heard about Dr. Becker's work. Panzer wrote Dr. Becker that his presentation was "the first startling new idea I have come across in many, many years," asked him to send a complete summary of his work, and encouraged him to submit a special grant proposal outlining the aims he had for future studies. Dr. Becker listed an array of studies and requested funds for a broad range of equipment including power supplies, signal generators, an electromagnet, data recorders, microscopes, a micromanipulator, and various instruments for measuring electromagnetic energy. He made no request for salaries for technical personnel, preferring instead to continue to work alone.

In July 1961 he presented a paper at an international conference on medical electronics in which he described what he said was his discovery of a previously unrecognized biological control system that consisted of a complex pattern of DC voltages which were generated within and distributed by cells in the central and peripheral nervous systems. The inputs to the control system, he said, were tissue trauma of any type including pain, radiation, and environmental electromagnetic energy. The system outputs were signals that controlled growth, tissue healing, level of consciousness, biological cycles, and possibly migratory behavior in animals. He told the audience that all the listed factors had been evaluated in a preliminary fashion, and that more in-depth studies were urgently needed. He also said that a link between electromagnetic fields and mental health had been uncovered, and that continuing work was confirming the initial results.

His comment concerning the fields interested several government engineers in the audience who had been working on controlled nuclear fusion, a project that involved use of strong magnetic fields. The engineers told Dr. Becker they believed the fields were safe because no detrimental effects on the workers had been seen but nevertheless, perhaps out of an abundance of caution, they invited him to present his research results at a conference at the Massachusetts Institute of Technology.

Years later, when he was closing his laboratory, while we were working together on a book about his research, I came across an articulately written version of his presentation and recognized that his conclusions had been the wellspring for much of his subsequent work. I talked with him at length about the meeting, sensing as I did the historical importance of his presentation.

"How many people were at the meeting?"

"I don't know exactly. A lot. I had no idea that so many engineers were interested in magnetic fields."

"What was their general attitude regarding the direction from which you were coming?"

"Like the mindset about the effects of nuclear explosions on troops. No one had given any serious thought to the long-term consequences of being exposed to the blasts. If you weren't so close that you got blown up or burned, or suffered acute consequences from the radiation, then you were assumed to be unaffected. It was the same with magnetic fields. The engineers saw no acute effects due to the fields, nobody turned green, so it was assumed that the fields were harmless."

"Why do engineers think that way?" I asked.

"You tell me," he replied.

"But you must have some idea?"

"I suppose they are afraid that precautionary measures might interfere with their work, so they just naturally set the bar very high. And I think the engineering mentality is focused on the here and now. When they flip a switch they expect that if anything is going to happen, it will happen immediately, not next year. Charlie Bachman told me what their attitude would be, that the earth's field was too weak to be detected by humans."

"Did he believe that?"

"Charlie was a practical guy, that's what I liked about him. He never claimed that something wouldn't work because he had an equation that said so. He told me equations can explain or predict, but they can't exclude."

"What did you hope to accomplish by your talk?"

"I just wanted the government to use common sense, to study whether what they were planning to do could have side-effects, and to do it before they built the device."

"Were there any other people at the meeting with outlooks similar to yours?"

"Only Frank Brown."

"What was your plan for your presentation?"

"More or less to follow a logical one–two–three order. First I told them that the literature of bioclimatology contained many attempts to relate psycho-physiological disturbances in the human population with various physical parameters of the environment, and that a few studies had dealt with magnetic fields. I knew what the major objection would be, that the mechanism of action was completely unknown. Even back then I knew the argument was engineering-speak for 'the claimed effects of magnetic fields were artifacts,' so my next step was to try to give reasons to revisit their assumption that electromagnetic fields couldn't be hazardous. I told them there was new evidence that had a direct bearing on the validity of their objections, particularly evidence regarding geomagnetic fields. I pointed to free radicals, semiconductors, conduction bands in tissues, and our work on an organized neural control system in vertebrates that in combination provided a mechanism whereby environmental electromagnetic fields could exert an influence on human beings. Then I described some of the reported effects."

"Which ones?"

"Lissman's work. If a fish could detect tiny electromagnetic fields, wasn't it reasonable to at least keep your mind open to the possibility that humans could also do it? Other examples were human detection of radar fields, protozoa that exhibited orienting responses to electromagnetic fields, and Frank Brown's work. Then I told them about the work that Howard, Charlie, and I had done. That it was a statistical study which related daily changes in the intensity of the earth's magnetic field that had been measured by the government at Fredericksburg, Virginia, to the daily rate of psychiatric admissions to the VA and Upstate hospitals over a four-year period. The two indices rose and fell together, suggesting the possibility of a cause-and-effect relationship."

"How was your presentation received at the meeting?"

"Well, let me put it this way. A hundred papers were presented, but when MIT Press published the proceedings, neither mine nor Brown's were included."

Dr. Becker had worked diligently to prepare his remarks. He felt honored to have been asked to make a presentation at what he considered to be the center of the world of science. He had been convinced he could tell a compelling evidence-based story that would be accepted and ultimately lead to a new age of discovery in areas that mattered most to him. But the reaction he received disappointed him. Reviewing the trajectory of his career as I was then doing, using only the wisdom and insight that I then possessed, I felt that his experience at MIT was a watershed moment for him, perhaps the first time he sensed that his journey wouldn't end well.

Saturday Review invited him to write an article that summarized his work for the layman. He ignored the advice of those who told him that the magazine was an inappropriate audience for a serious scientist. He was working far out on the boundaries of present knowledge, and he believed he had to explain his results in understandable terms that were acceptable to a broad range of scientists and clinicians as well as to interested laymen, and that was what he attempted to do. In experiments with salamanders and frogs, he said, he had detected and measured DC currents that flowed from and to the brain along the fibers of the nervous system. The current flowed in one direction along the sensory fibers that transmit detailed information to the brain gathered by the eyes, ears, nose, and skin, the information that allowed humans and animals to see, hear, smell, and feel pressure, heat, or pain. The current flowed oppositely along the fibers of the nerves that transmit information from the brain to the muscles to make them contract. Thus the novel electrical circuit had complementary halves formed by the two kinds of nerve cells. He had discovered, he said, the most primitive guidance system within man's body, the system through which the environment originally instructed our oldest ancestors regarding the behavior that was necessary to survive on earth. As evolution progressed, and animals grew more sophisticated, the nerve-impulse system that makes modern man a quick thinker and agile actor gradually took over some control functions. But the older, more basic data transmission system remains active, and the ability of nerves to convey sense and motor impulses depends on the presence of that primordial current. The implication, he said, was that there was a real physical basis that could account for the observed correlation between geomagnetic fields and the incidence of psychiatric disturbances.

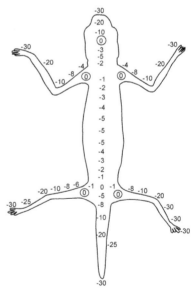

Results from "Bioelectric Field Pattern in the Salamander," published in 1960, showing measurements of DC voltage in millivolts. Circled areas show locations of nerve cell bodies. The results reflected the structural organization of the salamander's nervous system.

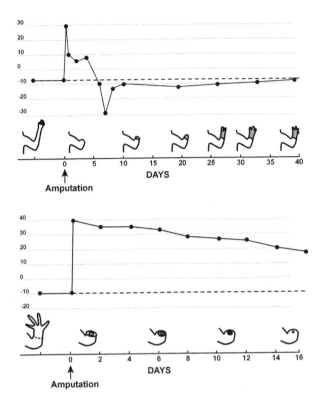

Results from "Biologic Factors in Amphibian-Limb Regeneration," published in 1961, showing measurements of DC voltage in millivolts at the end of limbs of sala- manders (top) and frogs (bottom) following amputation. The pattern differed markedly in the salamanders and only they grew new limbs.

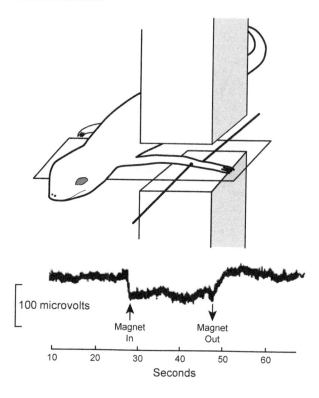

100 microvolts

Magnet
In

Magnet
Out

10   20   30   40   50   60

Seconds

Results from "Current Flow in Nerves of Salamander," published in 1961, showing the Hall effect signal measured in a living salamander.

Chapter 5.

Implications

————————•◦•————————

1962–1963: He makes further discoveries, receives additional national funding, continues publishing in prestigious journals, and explores the consequences of his theories

When Dr. Becker interpreted the results of the Hall study as evidence of a previously unknown neural current, he also accepted the idea that the current consisted of a flow of electrons because he had learned from Bachman that was the kind of current the Hall method detected. But the existence of an electron current as a means by which electromagnetic energy flowed through nerves was a jolting idea in the biological realm, quite at variance with the prevailing belief among experimental biologists that all currents in living animals consisted of ions moving in a watery environment, not electrons moving through something solid, as they do in a lamp cord. Dr. Becker further learned from Bachman that if a current in nerves were composed of ions, freezing the nerve would stop the flow of current because the ions would be locked in place by the low temperature. But if the current consisted of electrons, the laws of physics ensured that the current would increase. Dr. Becker froze small sections of a nerve in an anesthetized salamander and observed current increases, which he took to mean that electronic currents were flowing in nerves. When he published his results he cited Albert Szent-Gyorgyi who, years earlier, had also proposed that electrons could flow through tissues. That proposal had been strongly criticized by physicists, who knew far more about currents than he. Dr. Becker resurrected the theory, but without considering the arguments made by Szent-Gyorgyi's critics that the flow of electrons through tissues was impossible.

Szent-Gyorgyi was a physician who worked mostly in research. Toward the end of his career, long after he had won his Nobel Prize in biochemistry, he began speaking and writing about the insufficiency of biochemistry to yield an understanding of health and disease. His quest for answers drove him to concentrate on the behavior of moving electrons, which he suspected were the fundamental reality of life, the subject that then interested him the most. During a dinner one evening, which occurred many years after the period in Dr. Becker's work that I am now describing, Szent-Gyorgyi explained his perspective to me. He held out his hands, palms up, like cradles, looked at his left hand and said, "dead rat," and then at his right hand and said, "live rat." He gently bounced his hands as if to allow me to gain an appreciation of the distinction between the two states of being, saying, "What is the difference between the rats? Not biochemistry, because the biochemicals in both are the same."

I asked what he thought the difference was and he told me it was electrons moving in the living animal that coordinated spatially separated biochemical reactions. He wasn't downplaying the achievements of biochemistry, only saying that life didn't exist at the biochemical level but rather emerged from complex combinations of myriad biochemical reactions that were controlled and integrated by the flow of information. When I returned to Syracuse I asked Dr. Becker the same question, and he gave me more or less the same answer.

Dr. Becker had begun his research career with the same attitude Szent-Gyorgyi had developed after he became famous, that biochemistry could not explain biological phenomena that occurred over a distance rather than just at a particular location, and that could last for days or weeks rather than just for a moment, phenomena that Dr. Becker called growth control, physiologists called regulation, physicians called healing, psychologists called behavior, and philosophers called consciousness. Awed by the mysterious ways of living systems and struck by the inadequacy of conventional biological concepts and experimental methods to explain them, both men had begun considering a role for electromagnetic energy, and both had become fascinated with the idea of energy transport by means of electrons. Szent-Gyorgyi had become mired down with a focus on a few types of mobile biomolecules in which he believed electrons bounced back and forth over short distances like balls in a pinball machine. Dr. Becker's electrons, in contrast, moved everywhere in the patient, perpetually making round trips through the nerves. He proposed the idea to help make his control-system approach tangible so that it would be properly considered, not dismissed unthinkingly as the local research committee had done when it first considered his research proposals. He had recognized that he needed to support his message with a story about how biological control could work. "That's what Szent-Gyorgyi should have done," Dr. Becker once said to me, "then he might have won another Nobel Prize."

As it happened, the moment was ripe for Dr. Becker. A Frenchman named Léon Brillouin had provided a theoretical explanation for how electronic current moved through wires. His model allowed electrons from the metallic atoms to pass through an energy highway inside the metal called a "conduction band," resulting in a "conduction current." Transistors had been invented, and they also passed electrons through a conduction band, but those electrons mostly came from foreign atoms that had been added to the transistor material, a process called "doping," rather than from the material itself. When the conditions were right, electrons liberated from doping atoms moved through the transistor, a form of electronic flow that became known as semiconduction. According to Brillouin's theory, nerves could not pass a conduction current, but the possibility existed for a semiconduction current if it were the case that nerves contained doping atoms. Thus the general movement of ideas and experimental methods in solidstate physics had provided Dr. Becker the necessary support to hypothesize that electronic current could flow in nerves by means of semiconduction. He told me that when he took that bold and unprecedented step he was acutely aware of his limitations as an experimentalist in solid-state physics, but that the developing shape of his project essentially forced him to do so. He explained that the current he had discovered wasn't ionic, and there were no wires in nerves to allow a conduction current. Semiconduction was the only other possibility.

While working essentially alone, normal for him, and struggling to find the experimental evidence he needed, Fred Panzer called and told Dr. Becker that Central Office would fund his research. "How much?" Dr. Becker told me he asked Panzer. "Whatever you need," was the reply. A surgeon at another VA hospital who knew Dr. Becker and was familiar with his work told me about the advice he had given Dr. Becker regarding the grant. "If you continue to work as you have done in the past," he said, "you will have the time to learn about the areas of science where you weren't trained but that are important for your work. Small budgets mean small responsibilities and less pressure to succeed, so the environment would be conducive to minimizing errors. Accepting the money from Central Office will result in new responsibilities and distracting demands." He advised Dr. Becker to turn down the funds from Central Office and remain on his present course, supported only by local funds. The advice shocked Dr. Becker and he resolutely rejected it. "I could not possibly do that," he told the surgeon.

He purchased equipment designed to study semiconduction. His major acquisition was a "paramagnetic resonance spectrometer," a complex instrument that could detect the doping atoms which he supposed were in nerves. He also purchased an "emission spectrometer," another instrument that could detect doping atoms, by burning the samples and then analyzing the colors of the light in the flame. After learning that the presence of water could enhance semiconduction and that measurements of the dielectric constant of tissue could be used to ascertain how much water it contained, he bought an instrument for measuring dielectric constants.

In preparation for experiments using the paramagnetic resonance spectrometer, he harvested frog sciatic nerves. After drying them, a step required for examining any material in the spectrometer but a harsh treatment for nerves, he positioned specimens in the middle of a microwave cavity located in a magnetic field. He expected the putative doping atoms to cause a change in the microwaves when he slowly changed the field strength, thereby generating a signal detectable by the instrument. But he detected nothing from the dried nerves, which looked like crinkled slivers of straw, leaving him to wonder whether that was because there were no doping atoms or there was some other explanation. He made no immediate use of either the emission spectrometer or the dielectric apparatus because the sample-preparation techniques required far more time and effort than he had anticipated. Instead he requested additional funds from Central Office to hire some of the graduate students who worked in Dr. Bachman's laboratory. The two men agreed upon a plan whereby the students would carry out experiments as their dissertation research under Bachman while working in Dr. Becker's laboratory and using his instruments.

You might expect that Dr. Becker's research progress would have earned him much local acclaim, but that wasn't what happened. The hospital director had initially become wary of him when Central Office began funding him directly and then intervening locally in his favor such as by ordering that he be given more space for research. The director saw research as more or less a hobby rather than something that might ultimately benefit veterans, and he aimed a range of subtle antagonisms at Dr. Becker. Robert Chodos, the chief of the research service, recognized Dr. Becker's rising tide of publications and asked to "join your research team," a request Dr. Becker saw as a demand by an administrative superior to be listed as an author on his publications. He angrily refused and the resulting mutual enmity became palpable and permanent. When they passed in a hallway or shared an elevator, they would each stare ahead icily without the slightest acknowledgment of each other's presence.

Dr. Becker was publishing more papers with less funding in journals with greater prestige than any of the investigators who worked in the medical school. And even more galling to them, his work was guided by considerations of electromagnetic rather than chemical energy, which made him too strange to merit their respect. So he continued his work in the absence of any collaboration. His attitude of doing things his way irrespective of the opinions of others only exacerbated the negative feelings toward him.

When he had reflected on the Hall study, he realized that the internal electromagnetic energy system essentially amounted to a previously unrecognized pathway by which the environment could affect the body. This had to be true because the energy flow inside the salamander had changed when he applied an external magnetic field. He had reasoned that natural external electromagnetic signals could also affect the internal energy system, and that such changes must have biological consequences because the internal system was the body's natural regulatory process. That intuition was so profound that even today many people still cannot grasp it. In November 1962 he gave his first detailed explanation when he presented a talk entitled "Semiconducting Biological Control Systems and their Interactions with Magnetic and Electric Fields" at a meeting of the New York Academy of Sciences. He began by telling the audience he would describe experiments that supported the idea of a link between a control system he had discovered and electromagnetic energy, both natural and man-made. He said, "Standard concepts of the structure and function of living cells and organisms do not include any mechanism that could allow an interaction with electromagnetic energy to produce detectable biological changes." It is important for the reader to realize the novel conceptual distinction that Dr. Becker had made. Intense levels of electromagnetic energy had long been known to cook tissue and to produce an effect uniquely associated with living animals, called "shock," which could range in physiological intensity from minor unpleasantness to electrocution. Taken together, he said, the DC voltages, the Hall effect, semiconduction, Twitty's salamanders, Brown's worms, and the results of his own psychiatric studies implied the existence of a class of effects that occurred only in living tissue, caused no conscious sensation, but nevertheless produced subliminal physiological consequences. No other investigator had made this distinction so vividly, incorporated it into his work so fundamentally, or provided as much theoretical and empirical evidence as he did, even though his career had only just begun.

He told the audience he had found evidence that electronic currents flowed continuously in the central and peripheral nervous systems, a process he called semiconduction, that the currents mediated important body functions including growth, healing, and consciousness, and that changes in the currents produced changes in function. He had sought experimental verification by studying the effects of artificial magnetic fields and DC currents on the electrical control system for consciousness.

He described measurements of DC voltages between the front and back of the head that he had made in worms, fish, salamanders, and man. Across all these levels of life, the front was negative in relation to the back, and the strength of the voltage decreased progressively as the depth of anesthesia increased, regardless of the anesthetic agent employed. If, as he had supposed, the DC voltages controlled the level of the brain activity that produced consciousness, then externally applied electromagnetic energy should alter consciousness. When he applied DC voltages to salamanders in a manner designed to reduce the naturally present voltage between the front and the back of the head, the animals became unresponsive to painful stimuli and exhibited electroencephalograms resembling those associated with deep sleep. Thus, as predicted, he had produced a decrease in the level of consciousness by artificially inducing a reversal of the normal DC voltage across the head. Then, even more remarkably, he got the same result when he applied magnetic fields. The electroencephalogram at the start of the experiment showed the normal pattern for an awake salamander. As the magnetic field strength was increased a particular pattern appeared, called a delta wave and generally known to indicate deep sleep, and the animals became unresponsive to painful stimuli. When the magnetic field was removed the normal pattern in the electroencephalogram promptly reappeared. He concluded that "external electromagnetic fields can profoundly influence the basic functional level of the central nervous system, leading to clinical consequences."

Following his presentation there was a question-and-answer period, which was recorded, as was the custom of the Academy in those days. He was asked whether the magnetic field effects might be marginal, considering that some of them had occurred only at high field strengths. "One must keep in mind," he replied, "that the effect was a very gross one, namely the production of a state of general anesthesia. Might it not be possible that much smaller fields, properly modulated, could produce physiological or functional effects of a much more subtle nature?" He reinforced the point by citing Brown's work and his own work with Friedman concerning hospital admissions for schizophrenia. Nevertheless the questioner persisted, "Suggestions that geomagnetic fields influence our behavior seem untenable in the face of the magnitude of man-made magnetic disturbances that we seem able to tolerate." Dr. Becker replied, "The questioner did not in any way refute our published work regarding a highly significant correlation between these two variables. I would certainly appreciate any specific comments he has in this regard."

He was challenged on the claim that the DC voltages he had described in his *Science* article were true Hall voltages. His questioner asserted that the claim was "insufficient from the standpoint of physics," but added, "Since no satisfactory explanation is available, even the refuting of the author's views should lead to new insights."

Another commentator said that Dr. Becker had "failed to support his speculations," and that he should "present observed semiconductor properties of the brain with calculations of the magnitude of the effect that could be produced in tissue." Dr. Becker called the suggested calculations "absurd" because "calculations can produce any desired result, depending on the assumptions employed."

Having performed such calculations myself many times, I can attest that Dr. Becker's reply is indubitably true. He somehow knew that truth but I never understood how he knew it because he was very far from being a mathematician and therefore quite incapable of directly verifying the reliability of what he had said. It's a dangerous thing for a man to claim scientific knowledge in the absence of empirical evidence. But during many years working for him I saw him do it successfully several times, which ultimately led me to conclude that not all reliable scientific knowledge is the product of the scientific method. There exists in the human mind a power akin in its provenance to religious belief. Call it what you may. I call it intuition. No one I ever knew personally had that power to the degree he did.

While he was confronting the problem of how to design experiments that would furnish more evidence of semiconduction in nerves, he met Andrew Bassett, a crafty orthopedic surgeon from Columbia University who was then conducting research into a particular form of bone growth. When a fractured leg bone is not treated with proper immobilization, it may heal with an angle in the middle of what nature intended to be a straight bone. But if a patient with such a crooked bone walks on it, sometimes new bone forms on the concave side of the angulation, which is under compression during walking, and existing bone resorbs from the convex side, which is under tension during walking, ultimately resulting in a straight bone. This change in bone architecture, called "modeling," is only one example of the general principle that mechanical forces strongly influence the growth and shape of bone, a principle that had long been known, although the underlying control system was unknown.

Bassett had learned from Dr. Becker's work that the end of a regenerating salamander limb was electronegative, and he wondered whether the concave side of a bone angulation, the location where new bone grew, might also be electronegative. Dr. Becker was invited to speak at a national meeting of orthopedic surgeons where he and Bassett discussed the possibility that electrical signals in bone might explain its modeling behavior. The idea resonated with Dr. Becker and he became interested in determining whether bone produced DC voltages, which he regarded as the indicators of the currents that mediated biological growth. They agreed to do cooperative studies, each working in his own laboratory.

They clamped bone specimens at one end and bent them by applying a force at the other end, and found that voltages appeared on the bone surfaces. Sometimes the voltages appeared and slowly decreased as time passed, and when the force was removed a voltage appeared in the opposite direction that quickly decreased to zero. Other times a pair of symmetrical voltage pulses appeared momentarily, one when the force was applied and a second when the force was removed. In a report submitted for publication in *Science* they each emphasized what they considered important. The story for Dr. Becker was that the voltages from bone lasted as long as the force was applied. For Bassett, who focused only on the symmetrical pulses, the important point was that the areas of compression were electronegative. The only conclusion they agreed on was that bone could transform mechanical energy into electrical energy. A peer reviewer mentioned that prior work published in Japan had shown that bone was piezoelectric, meaning that it could generate a voltage when subjected to mechanical forces. The reviewer's comment surprised Dr. Becker twice; that bone was already known to be able to generate an electrical signal, and that Bassett seemed to have already known that was the case.

The report was published in *Science* and three months later Bassett received a letter from an assistant professor of engineering at MIT named Dean Karnopp, who indicated his interest in cybernetics and raised a question regarding how paired pulses could serve as a control signal for bone modeling. Since they were symmetric, he said that whatever biological signal was sent to cells at a particular location in bone by one of the pulses would tend to be cancelled out by the other. Bassett told Karnopp that there were many ways a symmetric pair of pulses could produce a directed biological response, but in a letter to Karnopp and Bassett, Dr. Becker disagreed with both of them. Bassett was wrong because what Dr. Becker called a "zero-sum" signal could not function as a biological control signal, and Karnopp was wrong because the measured voltages were not symmetric, as could plainly be seen by looking at the figures in the *Science* article. Because the voltages were not symmetric, their origin had to involve more than just ordinary piezoelectricity.

At an international congress on zoology in August 1963, a week-long affair that involved hundreds of speakers and thousands of attendees who discussed every aspect of experimental biology, during a forty-five minute presentation Dr. Becker described the full dimension of his work on the neural growth-control system. In the session where he spoke, Lenicque from the University of Stockholm described the chemical composition of tissue extracted during the early development of the chick embryo; Wolff from the College of France discussed biochemicals involved in the regeneration of fresh-water worms; Rose from Tulane University talked about the factors that helped determine why the head of an animal begins to form in the embryonic stage of development where it does rather than someplace else in the embryo; and Bloch from the University of Texas used a method of chemical dyes to show that the DNA from diverse species was nearly identical. Then in a breathtaking elevation in scope and significance, Dr. Becker described his discovery of a new communication system in the body that controlled its growth and behavior. He told the audience that all living organisms possessed to one degree or another the property of self-repair, and that its major characteristic was what he called its "relatedness" to the total organism, by which he meant that the new tissue was particularly appropriate to replace the missing part. The new tissue was somehow furnished by the organism with information that controlled the tissue's exact location and composition. Additionally some kind of an error-sensing process ensured that the structure of the new tissue actually fit the organism's requirements. This meant that there needed to be a two-way communication between the new tissue and the organism itself. This communication system was necessarily primitive because it was a basic attribute of all living things, and consequently had to be in place prior to the evolutionary developments that allowed living things to do more than simply self-repair.

In other words, the overall regulatory system necessarily had a monitoring function by which the organism continuously recognized the presence of normalcy, a sensory function by which it determined when and where deviations occurred, an effector function by which it initiated appropriate repairs, and a feedback capability by which the effector function was continuously diminished in proportion to the extent of the repair that had been accomplished.

He then reviewed the results he had published in *Science*, *Nature*, and top journals in bioengineering and medicine and concluded that the nerves of animals and humans generated and transmitted small steady electronic currents that amounted to a primitive, physical, analog communication-and-control system by which the organism knew itself, responded appropriately to trauma, and detected electromagnetic energy in the organism's environment.

Several objections to various parts of his talk were raised by persons in the audience, but he told me they involved only small details and that he considered his presentation on the world stage as having been successful.

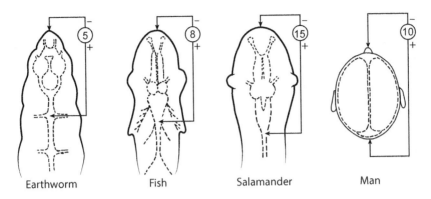

Measurements of DC voltages (in millivolts) across the brains of animals and man. Presented at a meeting in New York in November 1962.

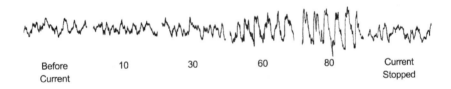

| Before Current | 10 | 30 | 60 | 80 | Current Stopped |

Measurements of the effect of artificially produced DC current (microamperes) on the electroencephalogram of a frog that occurred at the indicated time (minutes) after current flow began. Presented at a meeting in New York in November 1962.

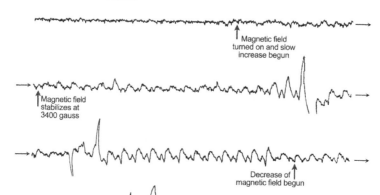

Measurements of the effects of artificially produced magnetic field on the electroencephalogram of a salamander. The large excursions are movement artifacts. Presented at a meeting in New York in November 1962.

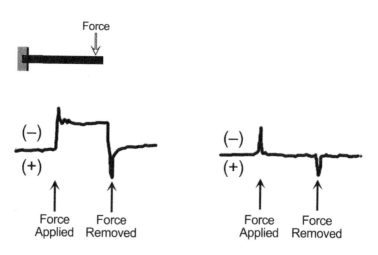

Measurements of the piezoelectric effect in bone by Drs. Becker and Bassett. From "Generation of Electric Potentials by Bone in Response to Mechanical Stress," published in 1962. Time-dependent voltages recorded by Dr. Becker (left) and Dr. Bassett (right) following application of force to a cantilever-mounted bone specimen (top)

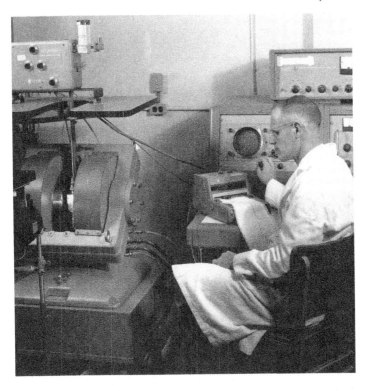

Dr. Becker operating his paramagnetic resonance spectrometer in 1963.

Chapter 6:

Controversy

1964–1965: He concentrates on bone research, wins a national research award, has a falling-out with a co-investigator, and becomes involved in a dispute about the electrical properties of bone

When Dr. Becker began his research, biology had more or less completed a transformation from a descriptive activity to an experimental science devoted to the systematic study of biochemicals. The prevailing orthodoxy saw all phenomena exhibited by living systems as results of connected series of biochemical reactions, like gears in a machine, and regarded the goal of research as the discovery of these reactions and the identification of their roles in a hypothetical linear causal chain. How reactions coordinately produced complex phenomena like healing or consciousness was not regarded as a serious question for study by the methods of experimental biology, and nil scientific efforts aimed at addressing the question were in progress. Dr. Becker thought that the emphasis on biochemistry was extreme to the point of self-contradiction because molecules weren't alive. He sought recognition of the idea that a system-wide perspective was also needed to help explain the complexity of human vivacity in health and disease.

He tried to elaborate a rudimentary holistic theory based on semiconduction in nerves, a process that would allow instant communication of energy and information between regions as far apart as the head and the toe without any need for intermediate biochemical reactions. Semiconduction was a well-established scientific concept, and it afforded the possibility of explaining how system-wide coordination could occur in living organisms. He felt he was on the right track and making progress, but when he had tried to support the idea of semiconduction by finding doping atoms in nerves he was unsuccessful. Even more troubling, he had no clear idea of the specific experiments he should perform to sustain his prodigious momentum. He was foreclosed from directly studying living nerve cells because he lacked the necessary specialized training and technical support. The alternative, studying dried dead nerve cells, offered scant hope of revealing useful information regarding how living cells functioned. During this period of hesitancy and uncertainty, traits that were highly uncharacteristic for him, he met Andrew Bassett. Following their successful collaboration that led to the discovery of stress-induced electrical signals in bone, they continued to work together, doing different kinds of experiments in their respective laboratories as befitted their differing inclinations and values.

Bassett's experiments were governed entirely by the biochemical fashion of the day, expanded only slightly to allow a modest role for electromagnetic factors. He was interested in how bone formed, which for him did not extend beyond answers to the questions of what biochemical stimuli activated bone cells, what nutrients they required, and what stimuli stopped the synthetic activity, questions that he and his staff pursued in his laboratory. He was an urbane, sophisticated man, and at the vanguard of a revolutionary change in orthopedic surgery that would ultimately transform it from the least to the most prestigious and profitable specialty in medicine. Because of his research prowess and his demonstrated successes in the area of medical economics, he was widely perceived to be on the fast track to becoming chairman of orthopedics at Columbia. Dr. Becker, in contrast, worked more or less in an intellectual vacuum, motivated by his ethical outlook concerning the proper role of a physician, and had no personal ambitions except to be credited for his discoveries.

Dr. Becker decided that the study of bone could be a principal path forward for his overall project. Bone was stable, solid, and for practical purposes contained no cells, a true material in the engineering sense of the term, not a biochemical, and readily available from his operating room. Its microanatomy had recently been discovered following the invention of the electron microscope, which provided dramatic images of uncountable tiny calcium-containing mineral crystals, all located in precise relation to slender fibers of a protein called "collagen" that coursed the length of the bone and strengthened it, like rebar in a column of concrete. The complexity of bone's structure seemed to him to offer the possibility that undiscovered physical properties of bone's constituents could help explain the mysterious processes that resulted in the creation of bone, and that permitted it to display its unique growth properties including mechanically driven adaptive growth and fracture healing, emergent phenomena, exactly the processes he sought to understand.

He never explicitly acknowledged a shift in the focus of his research. On the contrary, in his lectures and speeches he consistently said that his work on nerve and bone were two sides of the same coin, which was true only in the sense that they both involved considerations of electromagnetic energy. His publication record and his close connection with Bassett during the period I am now describing reveal the beginning of an intense focus on the question of how bone growth was regulated. He came to believe that the then-developing disciplines of medical electronics and biophysics and the use of new measurement techniques would lead to the answer.

His first attempt to find evidence of semiconductivity in bone involved using his paramagnetic resonance spectrometer to search for the presence of doping atoms. When he positioned human bone specimens in the microwave cavity of the instrument he observed a signal whose characteristics were exactly what he was looking for and had intended, if he found it, to interpret as evidence that bone contained mobile electrons from doping atoms, as in transistors. The results were published in *Nature*, though only after the manuscript was modified at the request of the editor to say that the observed signal could not "be definitely ascribed to a free charge-carrier population such as is present in doped semiconductors."

Over a short period, a matter of weeks perhaps, he developed an approach to the control of bone growth that was directly based on bone's electrical properties. He envisioned that an electrical signal from bone itself, caused by walking or the action of muscles, triggered cells on the surface of bone to produce new collagen scaffolding when and where needed to form new bone. A crucial consideration for him was the notion that the strength of the electrical signal was continuously reduced as the new bone was formed and ultimately disappeared when no more bone was needed. Thus what emerged from this thinking was the concept of a stimulus-response control loop for bone modeling based on negative feedback.

Because the mechanical forces on bone produced by walking or muscle action were periodic in the sense that they are continually applied and removed, he believed they were intrinsically unable to provide a cybernetic signal capable of directing growth. He resolved this perceived conundrum by asserting that bone allowed current to pass in only one direction, from the collagen protein into the calcium crystals. This process, called "rectification," occurred in a semiconduction device called a "diode," which consisted of two different semiconductors. Reasoning by analogy he con-cluded that the collagen and crystals were different types of semiconductors. Confident that he was on the right path, he described his ideas in a grant application to the National Institutes of Health and the grant was awarded, thereby enabling him to proceed with a broad range of biophysical studies. He received some advice from Bachman regarding various experimental details but otherwise worked alone.

He performed a series of measurements that would seem normal for a physicist working on transistors at Bell Labs, but that would be surprising if you learned that the measurements were performed by an orthopedic surgeon working on bone at a VA hospital. He studied photoconductivity, photovoltaic effect, action spectra, and recombination radiation in bone, and was spectacularly successful. Whatever shortcomings there might have been in experimental design, execution, or interpretation of data, they did not prevent his work from being published in world-class journals.

Dr. Becker supposed that the unidirectional currents in bone could cause the collagen molecules produced by bone cells to orient in the op-timal direction for forming the scaffolding upon which the calcium crys-tals were deposited to make bone. Bassett tested the supposition using a bench-top model system consisting of an acid solution of collagen molecules through which he passed an artificial current, and after only a few minutes he observed formation of a band of collagen at right angles to the current flow. Both men had a tendency to accelerate past the many nuances and limitations inherent in laboratory data and arrive at grand interpretations that had the power to grip the imagination. Unsurprisingly, each of them quickly construed the results of the study as compelling evidence for their narrative, that unidirectional currents in bone played a role in the bone-building process.

During the time Dr. Becker was performing his biophysical studies, he was also involved in studies on dogs that Bassett was carrying out in his laboratory. Bassett regarded voltage polarity as if it were a property of a location, like its temperature, rather than something relational like *up* or *down*. In this befuddlement he equated *negative* to *bone growth* and *positive* to *bone resorption*, and thus predicted that a DC voltage from a battery would make bone grow at the negative electrode and make existing bone resorb at the positive electrode, even in the absence of any mechanical stresses. He tested his hypothesis by inserting two wire electrodes into holes he had drilled into one of the leg bones in the dogs and connecting the wires to an implanted battery. Dr. Becker told me he had been certain that new bone would form somewhere, because electrically induced osteogenesis had been reported many times since the invention of the battery. He guessed the new bone would form somewhere along the path of the current in the marrow canal of the bone. As it happened, new bone grew at the negative electrode and existing bone resorbed at the positive electrode, as Bassett had predicted. In their report of the study, published in *Science*, they each held fast to what they believed, Bassett that electronegativity promoted bone growth, Dr. Becker that bone growth was the product of an electrical growth-control system.

During my first year in graduate school at Syracuse University, studying physics, I began working in Dr. Bachman's laboratory, tasked by him, for reasons I didn't understand, to measure DC voltages produced by goldfish. In the spring of 1964 he told his graduate students that a doctor at the VA hospital with whom he worked wanted to hire a graduate student for a project that involved "the physics of bone." I first met Dr. Becker when I interviewed for the job. He asked what I was doing in Bachman's lab, and why. I told him about the goldfish, and that I had no idea why Bachman wanted that data. Dr. Becker told me that "all animals have DC voltages on their surfaces that are related to their anatomy, and that change when injury occurs." I asked him where the voltages came from and he said from nerves and bone, and that they produced electronic currents, as in semiconductors. He talked about some of his research results and then said, "Man, perhaps, is more a creature of his environment than has been previously guessed." Before I could ask him what that meant, he asked me if I ever thought about what made something alive different from something that wasn't. I told him that the question had never come up in any of my classes and asked him what he thought the answer was. He said that the difference was the ability to self-repair, and that he was interested in how that happened. He described what he called his "biological philosophy," that the cell wasn't just a bag of water containing interacting biochemicals, but rather an organized solid through which electronic currents flowed, thereby transmitting energy and information to all parts of the body. Just before the interview ended he asked about my background and my plans for the summer. I told him that after college I had worked for a year as an engineer at an electronics company before returning to school so that I could delve deeper into physics, and that NASA had accepted me for a summer internship at Langley.

While I was at Langley he offered me the job in his laboratory. He chose me, I learned from him years later, because I seemed to be a "go-getter." When I started work in his laboratory he told me to design experiments on bone using the paramagnetic resonance spectrometer, to help support his semiconductor theory. He also said he wanted me to do experiments using the dielectric-constant apparatus, because the amount of water in bone was a matter of interest to him. I asked what kind of experiments he had in mind and he said the choice would be mine, with his and Bachman's approvals. At that time a technician named Fred Brown was the only other person working in the laboratory. Soon thereafter Dr. Becker hired a second physics graduate student, Joe Spadaro, and tasked him to use the emission spectrometer to find doping atoms.

About a month after I began work in his laboratory, Dr. Becker invited my wife and me to his home for dinner. He lived in the country, south of Syracuse, in a large house that overlooked an aspen grove. He showed me a trestle table he had built and smoothed by scraping with glass. He disdained the use of varnish and instead had finished the table with numerous coats of hand-rubbed oil. His artwork hung on the walls, a pen-and-ink drawing of a trout breaching a placid stream, a watercolor of a red barn, and an oil painting of the view from the picture windows in his living room. There were several woodcarvings, mostly pecan that he had shipped in from Louisiana and dried slowly by covering the logs with a blanket to prevent cracking. His wife, Lillian, who had an unfailingly present smile, asked me how I liked working for "Bob" and before I could answer she warned me that he could be "difficult," calling him "a stubborn Deutsche Mann." Whenever I asked him a question he gave a short, direct answer. Any details that I wanted always necessitated more questions. I struggled to frame questions that elicited answers describing how he knew the things he knew, questions that troubled me greatly because they seemed to portend the impossibility of closing the enormous gap in knowledge between us.

He operated two mornings a week, mostly procedures on the major joints and back fusions, and he saw patients in clinic in the afternoons. He worked in the laboratory later in the day, reviewing Fred Brown's work, making measurements, and writing notes. When he came into the laboratory the day before Thanksgiving in 1964 he was smiling.

"What happened?" I asked.

"I've been notified I'll receive the Middleton Award," he replied.

"What's that?"

"A national award that Central Office gives every year to the best research program in the VA."

"That's quite an honor," I said. "Congratulations."

"I published a lot, and in an area that's important. And I was fortunate because the awards committee considers non-biochemical projects. I guess my work didn't seem too strange."

"What exactly did they give you the award for?"

"It will say, 'for demonstrating that an electrical control system can be used to stimulate the regeneration of tissue in mammals.'"

Eiichi Fukada, a Japanese physicist who had discovered piezoelectricity in bone, came to Syracuse to meet Dr. Becker and discuss their theories regarding where the DC voltages in bone came from. Fukada was a soft-spoken, polite man who smiled frequently and easily as he explained his reasons for concluding that the piezoelectric voltages arose from collagen, bone's protein constituent. Dr. Becker told Fukada that he had little doubt that bone collagen was piezoelectric, but that he had been working on what he called "a somewhat different electrical effect" that better explained the origin of the DC voltages in bone.

"At present my thesis is that the DC voltage is generated by a functional unit in bone, a diode junction formed by the association of the mineral crystals with the collagen fibers. During the past year I have been able to substantiate the junction hypothesis by means of photoconductivity and other techniques. In all cases, bone behaved as predicted for a diode junction."

"I have one question," Fukada said. "Based on the diode mechanism, how do you explain the converse piezoelectric effect in bone, that is, the deformation that bone exhibits when I apply a voltage?"

"That probably occurs because the atoms in the vicinity of the junction are arranged very symmetrically," Dr. Becker replied.

"But there is no evidence that is the case," Fukada replied.

"Nevertheless," said Dr. Becker, "some artificial diodes used in sonar equipment follow this principle. Perhaps it also applies in bone."

"But in those cases, gallium arsenide is a good example, the mechanical distortion does not occur at a junction but rather in the semiconductor material itself. This explanation can be found in a book on acoustics edited by Mason that was published a few months ago. Therefore diode junctions in artificial crystals seem not to be applicable to the converse piezoelectric effect in bone, although I agree that there is no firm proof against the junction hypothesis in bone."

"I had the opportunity to speak with Dr. Mason this past January," Dr. Becker said. "He told me that piezoelectric phenomena in commercial semiconductors is still being investigated and new data being presented."

"That is true," replied Fukada, and Dr. Becker responded, "So at this time, both hypotheses are equally satisfactory and perhaps both are valid."

"Inasmuch as tendons also consist of collagen," Fukada said, "and I have shown that tendons are piezoelectric and exhibit both the direct and converse effects, would it not be simpler to say that the collagen in bone is the source of the DC voltages, and that perhaps any resulting current that flows is rectified by the junctional structure, thereby parsimoniously explaining the DC voltages while avoiding your concern regarding a zero sum signal?"

"At this time I do not believe that our views are incompatible and I feel certain that the two phenomena are related," Dr. Becker replied.

I thought at the time that Fukada's assessment was likely correct. After he departed I hoped Dr. Becker would discuss the issue with me but he didn't.

Dr. Becker spoke little of Bassett, and with an attitude that suggested past slights. I learned much about their relationship when Dr. Becker came to the laboratory late one afternoon, flushed with anger, and said, "Have you seen Bassett's article in the *Scientific American*?"

"No, I haven't," I replied as he handed me his copy of the October issue, opened to Bassett's "Electrical Effects in Bone."

"He stole my work, " Dr. Becker said. "He described the electrical control system concept and the negative feedback system for controlling bone growth as if it was his work, not mine. Even worse, he made it seem that the DC voltages were only a technological fix, something doctors might be able to apply to make you better."

"You don't think that's possible?"

"He obscured the important point of my work, to understand how the body works. Not to find a cure-all medicine. The electrical control system isn't a drug."

"Did you know he was going to send in the article?"

"He never said a word about it."

"Did you have any agreement with him about that?"

"We were supposed to keep each other up-to-date about our work on DC voltages. All publications were supposed to be jointly authored. He just lied to me. He says one thing but he does the opposite."

"Did he give you any credit at all?"

"Only to suggest that I was one of many who had made small contributions but that he was the one who saw the big picture. He listed my affiliation as 'Syracuse University,' even though he knows damn well that I work at the VA."

"Why did you get involved with him in the first place?"

"He had resources I didn't have. But I was doing fine without him. I didn't go to him. He approached me. He said my ideas would revolutionize biology. He asked for my help. I trusted him. Hell will freeze before I have anything to do with him again."

Dr. Becker's framework for the physical basis of the control system that governed bone modeling in response to stress was essentially free from open controversy, which may seem amazing to you because what he was proposing, why he was proposing it, and the evidence he was offering to support his arguments were all quite heterodox. But as I look back now I can see that the way his work was received at this point in his career was a predictable consequence of the forces in science that were then in play. His natural antagonists within experimental biology, Paul Weiss and Francis Schmidt, men whose work would be diminished were Dr. Becker's theory to become the new normal, were constitutionally cautious and proceeded ponderously, textbook by textbook, displaying little affection for new ideas that did not originate in their laboratories. They crafted incisive analyses of their own ideas, and of the responses from others that those ideas engendered, but their work was devoid of consideration of ideas generated by others. It was as if they thought that any attention to new ideas, even withering criticism, would generate publicity and possible interest. Both men met Dr. Becker at various meetings, and even participated with him in several panels, but they did not speak to him.

Among physicists his work was quite unpopular. They evaluated it the way they would the work of a physicist, by which I mean they were not predisposed to take into consideration the vastly greater complexity of living systems compared with the lifeless material they studied. Consequently they regarded his data as dubious and his interpretations as unwarranted. Moreover their philosophy did not encompass moral and ethical goals, but merely technical objectives, facts that made it even more difficult for them to see the value of his work. But little of the negative attitude of the physicists was communicated directly to Dr. Becker because he and they lived in separate worlds that did not overlap. He did not seek their opinion, they had no reason to volunteer it, and he probably would have ignored it had they done so. From the tone of some of the questions he was asked at various meetings, he knew of their hostility toward his work, and over time he honed his responses, which were almost always dismissive. One day following a presentation he made at a scientific meeting, someone in the audience asked him, "When you made the bone conductivity measurements, what kind of electrode did you use?"

"Aluminum," he replied.

"That was totally wrong. It is obvious that your results were artifacts because you used the wrong kind of electrode."

"What should I have used?" Dr. Becker asked, and the questioner said, "Platinum."

Dr. Becker replied, "I repeated the measurements using platinum and the results were exactly the same."

At a conference in New Hampshire his work was strongly criticized by a physics professor from New York University named Morris Shamos. When Dr. Becker told me the story he said Shamos was "didactic," and I could easily see from his tone and posture that he found Shamos more than a little irritating. The situation flared dramatically when Shamos published an article in *Clinical Orthopedics and Related Research* in which he roundly criticized every aspect of Dr. Becker's bone measurements. Shamos said that the DC voltages from stressed bone were mostly experimental artifacts, the data purporting to show the presence of a rectifier junction in bone was unreliable, the temperature dependence of the electrical current in bone actually showed that it was a semi-insulator, not a semiconductor, the paramagnetic resonance spectrometer results regarding the presence of doping atoms were not conclusive, and the photoconductivity results were thermal artifacts. For each claim, Shamos presented data that he said showed he was right and Dr. Becker was wrong.

Over several years I gained some insight into what had prompted Shamos to cross over from physics into orthopedics and criticize the work of someone who had crossed from orthopedics into physics. I will relate to you what I learned when I tell you the story of how Dr. Becker responded to Shamos.

According to the custom, Dr. Becker gave the keynote speech at the presentation of the Middleton Award for 1965. He chose "creativity in science" as his topic, particularly the problem of how science should "recognize the persons and ideas that have the potential of future value." He told the audience that it was important to consider "not only how we can identify and encourage creative persons, but also to identify the obstacles to achieving this goal that have been created by organized science itself." After pausing for a moment, he said slowly, "The very instrument by which creative thinking is communicated—the scientific paper—constitutes one such obstacle."

He argued that the separation of Results, called data, and Discussion, where theory, speculation, motivation, hypotheses, and meaning are recounted, "bore little resemblance to the actual sequence of intellectual and experimental events that went into the reported work." This format, he said, as enforced by journal editors and peer reviewers, allowed no insight into the all-important thought processes of the investigator, and substituted in its stead the misleading implication that truth emerged logically from data. The consequence was to reduce science to a mendacious activity because collecting data is a low-level activity, and even a dull-headed scientist could create a narrative Discussion for any set of data.

The scientific paper can be a barrier to creativity in other ways, he argued. Only unimaginative studies that contained no hint of promoting disharmony are likely to be found acceptable by the peer-review boards of the old established journals because the boards are biased in favor of the status quo. He said that no one could dispute the value of a paper that explained what was previously unexplainable, but "what about the reverse situation? I believe that a paper presenting data that renders unexplainable what was previously satisfactorily explained is equally valuable. Such destruction of cherished dogma formed the basis for modern science and we must always have a place for it—even today."

He concluded this line of thought by noting that the pressure on scientists to publish papers promotes mediocrity. "Most papers resemble pedestrian strolls through already well-cultivated areas by investigators playing the academic game of publish-or-perish." He said, "Anyone who succeeds in publishing a worthwhile paper earns our praises for having triumphed not only over nature but over the editorial review boards as well."

Then he proceeded to express opinions about the need to liberalize the present modes of scientific thinking about new concepts and theories. He said that most of the significant work in medical research was produced by scientists who had the ability to recognize the significance of apparently unrelated work reported by others and to apply it in an appropriate fashion to their own problems. He said that such "integrative mental processes" were "the hallmark of a creative scientist," but that equally important were the scientist's personal characteristics, particularly courage and intellectual curiosity. "A generous supply of the former is needed by any investigator who deliberately chooses to work in a field of research that has been little explored, where there have been no noble predecessors to set down guidelines and where one cannot predict with any degree of confidence that some publishable data will be obtained." He concluded, "The quality we call creativity may be composed of equal parts of serendipity, courage, and intellectual curiosity."

After hearing his presentation I felt I understood him better, although he still remained a puzzle to me.

Dr. Becker's name added to memorial plaque in VA central office honoring winners of the Middleton Award.

Chapter 7:

Dangers

1966–1969: He defends his semiconduction studies, presents evidence for a new theory of bone healing, becomes head of research at his hospital, expands his laboratory, and warns of environmental dangers

After working intensely and consulting occasionally with Bachman regarding the criticisms leveled by Morris Shamos, Dr. Becker published a full-throated response. He said that his semiconduction theory lent itself well to an explanation of the feedback control system governing mechanically induced growth and resorption of bone. He strongly insisted on the reliability of his data, mocked Shamos' attempt to distinguish between "semiconductor" and "semi-insulator" as a meaningless play on words, and criticized him for "an inexcusable misrepresentation of our data." Soon after his reply was published, a journalist from a popular science magazine interviewed Shamos, and the resulting article infuriated Dr. Becker because he felt it sanctioned the theft of his work and lies about it. He wrote the editor, "In the context of the advancement of scientific thought and ideas, there is no place for distortions of fact, deliberate omissions of information or other behavior that can only be attributed to desires for self aggrandizement."

I tried to talk to him about the Shamos situation.

"Shamos said that the controlling factor for bone formation was the piezoelectric surface charge rather than the DC voltage, which is what I remember that Dr. Fukada had mentioned. Do you think Shamos could be right?" I asked.

"No," he replied, "when we applied DC voltages to dogs, bone grew at the negative electrode, and as I told you earlier, negative voltages occur in areas of bone in compression, which is where bone grows. The connection is with DC negativity, which I can measure, not with surface charge, which can't be measured in live bone."

I said, "When dentists apply forces using wires, the part of the jawbone that's in compression resorbs, which is why the tooth moves in that direction. Doesn't that suggest that the type of stress isn't the basic signal

73

in the control system?"

"I don't think it suggests any such thing," he said in a tone that unmistakably indicated I should turn to other matters.

After a few months the controversy just died away. Dr. Becker went on to do his experiments, and Shamos returned to teaching.

Looking back now at the drama that unfolded, which helped reshape Dr. Becker's research efforts as I will soon describe, I can see more clearly what happened and why. Shamos had argued that the asymmetry in signaling Dr. Becker thought was needed for his control signal was actually present, but that he simply hadn't recognized it. Shamos had repeatedly emphasized that electrical charge was created on a bone surface whenever mechanical stress was applied, either positive or negative charge depending on the microarchitecture of the bone and the type of stress, and that the charge disappeared when the stress was removed. His point was that a perfectly respectable control signal capable of directing a biological response existed naturally in the body. Consequently Dr. Becker's assumption that a rectifying junction was needed to explain directed growth was a violation of Occam's Razor, the principle that the simplest satisfactory explanation was the best explanation. Further, Shamos argued, the junction concept also wasn't needed to explain either the continuation of the voltage during the time the stress was present or the presences of the second DC pulse because both phenomena were artifacts. They were actually created during the measurement process, and existed only when voltmeters were connected to the bone. Even Bachman had made this point, but not sufficiently forcefully I suppose.

Dr. Becker had argued that the results of his measurements, taken together, strongly supported his interpretations. He said that the hugely greater complexity of bone compared with transistors had to be taken into account when interpreting the data, and he criticized Shamos' failure to do so as well as his focus on tiny details and relatively trivial considerations. He saw Shamos as inventing arguments merely to win the debate, whether or not they were biologically relevant. Shamos repeatedly appeared to claim credit for work that Dr. Becker had done. Whether intentional or the result of inartful writing I cannot say, but Dr. Becker had no doubts. The idea that someone would do such a thing was always what he hated and feared most. He became angry whenever he perceived any instance of it, almost as angry as when he witnessed the abuse of a patient.

I repeated Dr. Becker's semiconduction measurements. Sometimes I got the same results he had reported, and sometimes I didn't, which was reasonable, I thought, because no two pieces of bone are identical, in stark contrast to the indistinguishability of the transistors that come off an assembly line. When I told him what I had done and what the results were, he nodded as if to say that was what he expected if his experiments were redone. He cautioned, "We can't keep doing the same experiment over and over again. If we did, how long do you think I would continue getting grants or getting papers published?"

For weeks thereafter I was troubled that he might have thought me disloyal, but my fear turned out to be groundless. Emboldened by the way he had received my efforts; I began a replication study of Bassett's experiment that had shown DC currents could orient collagen molecules in solution and induce them to form a band. Although I got the same result, I ultimately found that band formation resulted from a change in the pH of the solution brought about by electrolysis of water, a process that could not occur in the body in response to the natural DC voltages. Consequently Bassett's results actually furnished no evidence to support Dr. Becker's growth-control system. When I told him what I had done, his countenance was more or less the same as when I had told him of my attempts to replicate his semiconductor measurements, perhaps with a somewhat increased level of acquiescent understanding. I wrote a report describing what I had done and concluded that DC currents in the body could in principle be responsible for organizing the structure of bone, as Dr. Becker and Bassett had supposed, but that Bassett's observations were not supporting evidence for the theory. I gave both men a copy of the report; Dr. Becker made some improvements and we published it. Bassett refused to contribute to it and join us as authors.

I wanted to repeat the Hall study, which Dr. Becker regarded as keystone evidence supporting his theory that weak electromagnetic energy in the environment could affect animals and human beings because the signals interacted with natural electrical regulatory systems in the body, what he called "the link between man and the environment." Objections had been raised against the study based on a variety of alleged experimental errors, some flagrant, and some inconspicuous. I had listed them and planned to evaluate them one by one in the expectation that his basic conclusion would be vindicated. I showed him the list and asked for permission to buy some salamanders.

"I've done all these things," he said. "Read my paper. It makes no sense to do them again."

"The objections were raised after the paper was published," I replied, "so it seems that they were not answered well enough."

"Some people will not believe a result they don't like, regardless of the evidence. The best way to deal with such people is to ignore them. They are always there, and they are unpersuadable. Did you find anyone who repeated my study and got a different result?"

"No."

"When you do, then you can buy the salamanders."

In a series of measurements designed to clarify the relation between force applied to bone and the piezoelectric charge that appeared on its surface, an engineer at West Virginia University named James McElhaney had applied force to a dried human femur and measured the resulting electrical charge that appeared on each square centimeter of the bone surface. Under an assumption that the cellular signal in Dr. Becker's growth control system actually was surface charge, we redrew the outline of McElhaney's femur, moving each measurement location to the left or right depending on the strength of the charge, whether it was positive or negative, and on whether the local stress was tension or compression. If the charge were unrelated to growth, the resulting outline should have appeared random, unrecognizable as a bone. But we found was that the outline of the bone shifted coherently, as if cells that would have been present on the surface of the bone if it were still in the body had built or resorbed bone according to the strength and polarity of the charge. The net effect was that the femur outline rotated to a new position where it could better resist the applied force, which was good evidence of a link between piezoelectric charge and control of bone growth. Dr. Becker cautioned against attaching too much significance to the result because there was far more evidence to indicate that the DC voltages were the cellular signal. Nevertheless he was pleased when our report about the study was accepted for publication in *Nature*.

Dr. Becker continued to support my PhD research project and that of

Joe Spadaro, even though the experiments we designed using the resonance and emission spectrometers and the dielectric apparatus had no direct relationship to his ideas about growth-control systems and environmental influence. We were preoccupied with the need to satisfy the requirement of our dissertation committees that our work be what they called "real physics."

From time to time the strangeness of the situation in the laboratory wafted into my consciousness. Dr. Becker seemed almost heroic in his dedication to his patients and to research. He had ideas about medicine and biology that almost took my breath away and a wondrously equipped laboratory in which almost anything any of us on his staff wanted was available or could be obtained. But the various ongoing projects were neither well synchronized nor focused to support his ideas, which seemed to me to be an inefficient use of his resources. But I did not dwell for long on the matter because I had little interest in changing the ground rules.

Dr. Becker's thinking regarding what experiments he would do moved away from semiconduction measurements and toward efforts seeking an understanding of the biological details of how electromagnetic energy controlled regeneration. This shift in emphasis was neither plainly announced nor apparent, but rather became clear only little by little. The first evidence of the shift that I recognized was the day he told us he intended to study the cellular aspects of the relation between DC voltages and fracture repair in frogs.

He manually broke the lower limb and measured the DC voltage that appeared daily following the injury. He sacrificed some animals each day and recovered the injury sites, which our technicians treated with formalin, embedded in wax, cut into thin sections, and stained with specialized dyes that permitted him to see the cells. His initial aim was to record the timing of the appearance of the bone-building cells and relate it to temporal changes in the DC voltages. He expected to observe a correlation, and planned to argue that the DC voltages had triggered bone cells to multiply and begin building new bone. The objective was audacious because everybody who cared about how bone cells were recruited believed that the injury-generated signal was a not-yet-identified biochemical agent. The source of the new cells, however, was not in doubt according to the common wisdom. The accepted view was that they came from the dormant cells on the bone surfaces that were activated by the injury. But to Dr. Becker's surprise he found no evidence in the microscope slides that the cells residing on the bone surface were dividing, implying that the new cells came from somewhere else. There was also another surprise, the appearance of odd-looking red blood cells at the injury site. His interest shifted from showing that the DC voltages activated the dormant cells to showing that the voltages actually made the bone cells from red blood cells.

When the conventions of experimental biology had first been established, Paul Weiss and his contemporaries taught that the process of cell development was irreversible, a one-way path, and that once a cell became committed to be a specific tissue, a process called "differentiation," the cell could not move back developmentally, a process called "de-differentiation" which, although it had a name, was held not to exist. No cell in the body was more committed to a specific role than was the red blood cell, whose obvious function in all animals was to transport oxygen. Notwithstanding the great weight of expert opinion to the contrary, Dr. Becker decided that frog red blood cells had de-differentiated, a notion even more heretical than his idea of electronic current in nerves and bone. His evidence for de-differentiation was the unusual cell shapes he found, which he showed matched perfectly the description that Johannes Holtfreter had published twenty years earlier when he described the normal developmental stages of differentiation of the frog red blood cell, except that the red blood cells in Dr. Becker's experiment went backwards developmentally, not forward.

One afternoon we talked about his experiments.

"Why do you care about where the bone cells come from?" I asked.

"Because Weiss and the others are wrong," he replied.

"Aren't you worried that trying to contradict them will be very difficult?"

"It's something that must be done. I can't accept whatever a supposed expert says just because he says it. Maybe he got his ideas in a dream or from a voice in a burning bush."

"But all the experts have evidence from their experiments."

"They think they have evidence, and they claim it's enough, but only because they ignore evidence that goes against their opinions. They must consider my evidence."

"Suppose they think your evidence is worthless, and not worth taking into account?" I said.

"Then the right thing for them to do is to say so, and explain why. Then others can judge who is right," he replied.

"Like with Shamos?" I asked.

"Exactly. He thought he knew about bone, but everything he said was wrong or half-baked and you can see what happened. My NIH grant was renewed, I got another NIH grant to train orthopedic surgeons in research, and his NIH grant was not renewed."

"It seems as if your big ideas about electrical control of fracture healing could be proved or disproved without talking about details like where exactly the cells came from," I said, only to be met by a grimace of the type that meant, "You just don't know anything about biology." Then he said:

"Suppose electromagnetic energy was responsible for the appearance of the cells at the injury site. Did you ever think about that possibility?"

"What do you mean?" I asked.

"Suppose the DC currents at the injury site de-differentiated the red blood cells, and caused those cells to re-differentiate into bone cells."

"That's a great idea, but how will you test it?"

"You'll see."

The next time he talked to me about his great idea he told me more about the motivation behind it.

"De-differentiation is a real phenomenon and its existence opens the door for explanations of many other things. The present dogma is wrong, and must be corrected."

"But it seems like an obscure topic, not of interest to many people," I said.

"If you had a better understanding of how tissue healed you wouldn't say that. If de-differentiation can occur in frogs, it probably can occur in humans. That means there is probably a way to create a pool of stem cells that can turn into any cell type and heal anything. It might be possible to grow a new joint, which would be far better than replacing a worn-out joint with a contraption made of plastic and metal. Perhaps it might even be possible to grow a new limb."

"But humans don't heal fractures by de-differentiation, you said so yourself many times, so it's hard to see why you press the issue."

"You missed the point. This project is not about fractures. It's about regeneration. Humans don't regenerate limbs. Why not? All of the elements of the regeneration control system are present except that we don't know which cell type has the latent power to de-differentiate and become a stem cell that could re-differentiate to form the cell types of the new tissue."

"Are you thinking that the red blood cell could be that cell type?" I asked.

With a sense of exasperation in his voice that made it clear that our conversation was over he said, "Of course not. The human red blood cell has no DNA so de-differentiation is impossible. It must be another type of blood cell."

For many months he worked in the back lab, where the frogs and microscopes were located. He said little about what he was doing, but I learned some details from Fred Brown, the only person who worked with him on the project. They obtained red blood cells from frogs that had not undergone any injury, suspended the cells in salt solution, placed a small amount of the solution into small plastic chambers positioned on the stage of the microscope, and passed DC currents through the solutions while directly observing and photographing the cells. Sometimes, when Fred performed the procedure and Dr. Becker was not present, I observed what happened. An ordinary red blood cell would go through a series of changes in its appearance, ending as a cell that looked nothing like a mature red blood cell. Not all of the cells changed and sometimes none did, and the amount of current needed to trigger the changes that occurred varied over an enormous range. These variabilities were explained away by Fred, who could only channel Dr. Becker, on the basis of many different factors, including age and/or health condition of the frogs, their hormonal status, and the extent of the stress that the frogs experienced during and after shipment from Tennessee, where they had been caught.

Several people who liked Dr. Becker but who had no inkling of his long-range plans urged him to move beyond amphibian research. They saw little reason to lavish time and resources on a matter as insignificant as how frogs healed fractures. He resented the unsolicited advice, which had an effect on his attitude opposite to that intended. Eventually he published a long report that contained numerous photomicrographs of red blood cells in various stages of de-differentiation at injury sites, the results of electrical measurements, and a variety of biochemical studies on the cells, all woven together in his unique narrative style that made it difficult to understand what evidence supported what statements, but that left no doubt about his overall message, that de-differentiation triggered by electromagnetic energy had occurred during amphibian fracture healing.

His publication rate and participation in scientific meetings began to decrease, and his heavy focus on the frog study was only one of the reasons. The pressure of his clinical duties increased relentlessly, particularly in the spring and summer months when travel in upstate New York was easier, resulting in overloaded orthopedic clinics. The hospital staff was expanding, and some of the newly hired physicians approached Dr. Becker for help in starting and maintaining their own research programs, a difficult task for a new investigator, especially when faced by a hospital administration that remained hostile to research. He helped where he could, but the bureaucratic difficulties with Chodos and the hospital director continued to aggravate him and others on the staff who, like him, had research projects funded by Central Office. Then one day Central Office asked Dr. Becker to accept the position of head of research at the hospital. He told me that one of the reasons he took the job was to eliminate the local projects that spent money year after year and produced nothing. But the least productive locally funded investigators were among the favorites of the hospital administration. He struggled to reform the system, but made more enemies than friends in the process.

Despite the leveling off of his research productivity, he enjoyed continuing success with his grant applications to the NIH and to Central Office, and the laboratory continued to expand. Biology PhD students and post-doctoral fellows joined the staff, and several additional technicians were hired. Orthopedic residents who contemplated a career in academics spent time in the laboratory to gain experience performing research. Typically someone coming into the laboratory interviewed with those already working there and then chose a project and a mentor. Dr. Becker would approve the projects and help if any serious problem developed, but only rarely did a new investigator work directly with him. One could learn from him by reading his papers, listening to his lectures, and by observing him, but in-depth give-and-take conversations with him rarely occurred.

One day in early 1967 I was surprised to learn that Howard Friedman had done human experiments involving the effects of artificial magnetic fields, and that Dr. Becker had been involved in the research. Their paper appeared in *Nature* and reported that magnetic fields had slightly delayed how quickly subjects could react to the appearance of a red light. When the opportunity presented itself I asked Dr. Becker about the study.

"I didn't know you were working on that."

"Howard wanted to follow up our work on schizophrenics," he replied.

"What was he trying to do?"

"We had shown that magnetic fields played a major role in keeping the DC system's control of body functions within normal bounds. Then Pokronoy published a paper that said Howard used the wrong statistics. That upset him, and he wanted to do more similar studies to show we were right, but I wasn't interested in getting sidetracked. Pokronoy is automatically against anyone who shows a link between any environmental factors and any disease. According to him, anybody who does must have used bad statistics. I told Howard to ignore him."

"Why did he do the reaction-time study?"

"You'll have to ask him that."

"Do you think it's a good study?"

"It might lead somewhere. You never know."

"That doesn't sound like a ringing endorsement," I said.

"I'm not a psychologist," he replied, ending the only conversation I ever had with him regarding the study, not because I wasn't interested in it but because I felt he wasn't.

Howard Friedman was a soft-spoken, reserved man who quietly went about his business as chief of the psychology service and, as time permitted, carried out research, but in a way that I suspected Dr. Becker believed was too ethereal. As the reader is probably aware by now, different kinds of investigators have different ways of designing experiments and making meaning from their investigations, and clinical psychologists were no exception. An opportunity to talk with Friedman presented itself when he asked me for advice regarding equipment he had assembled for generating magnetic fields.

"Why did you decide to study reaction time?" I asked.

"Bob wasn't interested in continuing the epidemiological studies on patients, so I decided to proceed with experimental studies. Turned out that he wasn't particularly interested in them either, but I went ahead and did them anyway."

"What is reaction time?"

"It's a standard uncomplicated psychomotor task that can tell us a lot about the way magnetic fields affect the brain."

"What did you learn from showing that that magnetic fields could affect reaction time?"

"That brain function can be directly affected by surprisingly weak magnetic fields, which was what first motivated Bob to suggest that we do the epidemiological studies."

"What will you do next?"

"I need to provide more evidence that my conclusions were correct and weren't due to artifacts or some kind of idiosyncratic choice of statistics. Unfortunately, I must do some animal studies before I can resume my human studies."

"Why?" I said. "You reported a pretty surprising and potentially important result. Aren't follow-up human studies essential?"

"I can't do more human studies until I evaluate the results of Russian investigators who reported that magnetic fields caused changes in the brain tissue of animals."

"Kholodov?" I asked. "Dr. Becker has mentioned him from time to time."

"Yes," he replied. "He said that magnetic fields caused a stress reaction that injured cells in the brains of rabbits."

I asked him what a stress reaction was. I knew the term "stress" only as a mechanical force applied to a material causing it to deform. But I understood from the context of our conversation that he was talking about some kind of biochemical change. He told me stress was a hormonal change triggered by environmental factors and that Madeleine Barnothy had reported that magnetic fields caused a stress reaction in mice. I knew of Barnothy, a physicist at the University of Illinois, because Dr. Becker had been in contact with her regarding matters he hadn't discussed with me. I didn't know anything about hormonal stress or Barnothy's research at that time, so I dropped the issue and returned to the Kholodov rabbit study.

"Do you think his work is believable? I suppose you know what Dr. Becker thinks about it."

"I can't ignore Kholodov's results," he replied. "I plan to repeat his study. If I don't find the effects he described, I'll be free to return to the human studies."

The equipment Friedman intended to use was designed to generate magnetic fields by means of the standard method, passing a current through a large number of loops of wire and allow the magnetic field from each loop to add so that the result was a field of substantial strength. Mostly he wanted to know from me whether the field of the coils he had built would be similar to Kholodov's field.

After I calculated an answer I returned to his laboratory and made some suggestions regarding the design and positioning of the coils so that the field would have more or less the same strength and direction everywhere in the region that would be occupied by the rabbit's head. I couldn't confirm that was what Kholodov had done because the translations of his papers were poor, but suspected that was the case and told Friedman so. Many years later, long after I had left Dr. Becker's laboratory, I met Kholodov in Russia and learned details about his experiments, including that my presumption had been correct. He also talked about field-induced hormonal stress, and credited Barnothy as the originator of the concept. I will have much more to say about stress later in my story.

Friedman asked me whether I had discussed his planned rabbit study with Dr. Becker, and I replied I had and that he wanted to be kept informed of the results.

"Why did you start to work with Dr. Becker?" I asked.

"He told me that DC voltages could be measured between the front and back of the head. I began measuring them and found that they became more positive during sleep, anesthesia, and hypnosis. It seemed as if the brain used the voltages to establish a hierarchic control over the autonomous systems in the body. I thought that if that were a general law, uncovering it would have great practical value."

"What happened with that project?"

"Bob was not interested in working on it. He had other ideas, and didn't want to spend the time needed to pursue studies of the nature and clinical significance of brain DC voltages. I understood that. It would be a lifetime project. I continued to work on the idea but progress has been slow."

"What happened next," I asked, "I mean with you and Dr. Becker?"

"He was interested in the effects of magnetic fields. Snails and worms and crabs all had been seen to respond to magnetic direction, and the fields have been reported to produce all kinds of behavioral effects. But no one knows the how or why of any of these effects. Behavioral psychologists ignored them, I think because of the absence of a theoretical framework that could explain them. Then Bob came along. His investigations into the electrical organization of living organisms led him to the idea that the DC electrical control system could be influenced by external magnetic fields. I got involved after he proposed to test his idea by performing a behavioral study of some of my patients."

"That was the first study you did together?"

"Yes, a pilot investigation of the relationship between changes in the earth's magnetic field and admissions to hospitals for schizophrenia, which is a gross manifestation of extreme psychological disturbance."

"Why schizophrenia?" I asked.

"Because a lot of people have the disorder and are admitted to the hospital for treatment. Bob knew I had access to the data. Epidemiological studies are a fertile field for providing insights into what to do next."

"I don't think he had ever done such studies," I said.

"True," he replied, and smiled as he said it. "Such studies are designed to find a correlation, in our case between schizophrenia and magnetic exposure. A correlation is a statistical fact, not something you can see or directly measure. Bob doesn't do statistics."

I told Friedman that I had read his report of the study that concluded the two parameters were correlated. He commented that the result didn't prove anything as far as he was concerned, but that it did appear to make worthwhile the task of trying harder.

"So what did you do?"

"I collected admissions data from seven hospitals, almost 30,000 patients. Even though use of hospital admissions is a crude measure of changes in human behavior, the results of the larger study were essentially the same as those of the first study."

"You got the same result?"

"In general, yes. The tentative conclusion of the pilot study was reaffirmed. There was a relationship between psychiatric disturbance as reflected in hospital admissions and changes in the natural magnetic field."

"Related in what sense?" I asked.

"The hospital admissions tended to occur one or two days after the geomagnetic field changed."

"That just seems amazing to me."

"I think it was. The results supported Bob's idea that the body has an electrical control system that can be affected by external electrical factors. But the meaning of the results was extremely limited. They were only correlations. Night and day are correlated, but nobody believes night causes day. They're both effects caused by something else. The results didn't provide any ideas regarding specific processes or mechanisms."

In August 1967 Dr. Becker was contacted by a congressman named Paul Rogers who was sponsoring a bill that authorized the U.S. Department of Health to perform research and regulate the safety of all radiation-emitting devices. Rogers wrote:

> It is my opinion that, rather than focus on one small segment of the radiation spectrum we must deal with the entire range and initiate intensive research in all frequency ranges in order that we may establish standards and control procedures while we are still in the early stages of the electronic age. I feel that if we begin studying the problem now before there is evidence of possible biological damage to large portions of the general population, we will be able to set standards—not through pressures of panic—but rather through the fruits of diligent and expanded research projects.

The letter pleased Dr. Becker enormously. He believed that determining what was harmful to the public before exposure was allowed to occur was the right thing to do, and that the electrical growth-control system could form the scientific basis for setting rules needed to protect public health. He wrote Rogers:

> I agree completely with your conception as outlined in the bill, and with your letter regarding the need for further study in the area and the requirement to provide a means of control over possible undesirable effects. We know that there are very definite biological effects with surprisingly small amounts of exposure. For example, in my own most recent work we have observed marked alteration in structure and function in certain cells with exposure of these cells to electric currents so small as to be at the limit of modern day measurement. It is quite possible that exposure to such current levels may arise inadvertently in the human population.

Rogers responded:

> I am most grateful for your statement of support for H.R. 10790. Although we are not faced with a great national radiation crisis, I, like you, believe that we must delve into this basically experimental field while it is still in the state of infancy. The enclosures describing your own work were most interesting. I believe these are areas of experimentation which

most laymen do not even know exist. Perhaps through your knowledge and experience in this area of low intensity electrical and magnetic fields, you might be able to comment on the potential hazards of unregulated and uncontrolled microwave radiation.

Rogers asked Dr. Becker to appear as a witness before his subcommittee, and to submit a statement expressing his support for the bill that expressed "any opinions which you might have concerning the hazards of random radiation." He agreed, telling Rogers that "I feel quite strongly that a start should be made in the direction of the finding of the areas of potential danger and instituting appropriate controls."

In the statement he submitted, Dr. Becker drew a parallel between ordinary semiconducting electronic devices and human tissue, particularly nerve and bone. In both cases, interaction with electromagnetic energy can interfere with normal function by "altering or stopping the flow of electrons" because that flow provided a control signal for a variety of basic functions. He said that electron flow in nerves determines the general level of activity of the nervous system, by which he meant how well it responded to stimuli and transmitted messages. The consequences, he said, would be changes in the rhythmic alteration of sleep–wakefulness in the system that senses trauma and initiates a response, and in the system that controls the cell growth necessary for healing. He conceded that the viewpoint of biological semiconductivity and its implications represented a considerable departure from classical biochemistry and physiology, but offered the judgment that "this concept while becoming more acceptable over the past ten years still has considerable opposition expressed to it because it has provided answers to questions that physiology and biochemistry have failed to solve." He argued that the earth's magnetic field was a physiologically important part of man's environment and that exposure to man-made fields, at both low and high intensities, either DC or at various frequencies, "may produce definite alterations in behavior and nerve function." In a strikingly prescient paragraph he warned about cancer.

"We have been able to take red blood cells from normal, non-fractured individuals and expose them to exceedingly small electrical currents and cause them to undergo the same alterations as in normal development. The importance of this observation, aside from the fact that it establishes that the healing of a fracture is produced by the electrical current stimulating the cells in blood clot, is that the cellular changes produced are very similar to the changes seen when a normal cell becomes cancerous. As a result, while we have been able to produce bone growth at will in animals by inserting appropriate small electrical currents, we have refrained from extending this technique to humans because of the danger of inducing an uncontrolled, or cancerous, growth. However, by the same token we may predict that effective control over cancerous growths may result from further understanding of this semiconduction system."

His basic point was that man-made electromagnetic energy in the environment would produce minute electrical currents within the body that might stimulate certain target cells to undergo transformations normally associated with healing mechanisms. Since there would be in this case no actual injury to heal, the normal control system would not be operative so there was the possibility that the altered cells would undergo unrestricted growth. He concluded, "I therefore feel that further research in the area of interactions between tissues and various types of external electromagnetic energy is necessary."

Other investigators submitted statements regarding X-ray devices, microwaves, sunlamps, lasers, and cell phones, but their mode of argument was not even remotely similar to that of Dr. Becker. Karl Morgan, a physicist at the Oak Ridge National Laboratory, said that X-rays were dangerous because they could disrupt DNA, which even the industry experts accepted. Regarding microwaves, which lacked the energy necessary to disrupt DNA, a veterinarian from the University of Rochester named Sol Michaelson described experiments in which he put dogs into what amounted to a large microwave oven and found that they didn't die until their body temperature went above 107° F. He said that as long as their temperature remained below that level, the dogs could "handle the heat." Herman Schwan, an engineer from the University of Pennsylvania, submitted calculations that he said showed to a mathematical certainty microwaves were perfectly safe for human exposure as long as they didn't produce the cooking effect demonstrated by Michaelson.

Political arguments concerning the bill lasted a long time, and the version that finally became law severely disappointed Dr. Becker because the principle of evaluating the health impact of radiation prior to marketing devices that produced electromagnetic energy was rejected in favor of the rule that consumers who claimed they had been injured would be required to prove that the device was unsafe. Five years earlier, following a scandal involving the drug thalidomide, federal drug laws had been amended to require drug companies to prove the safety of their drugs prior to selling them. Dr. Becker strongly believed that the same principle should have been applied to the side-effects of radiation, but that was not what happened.

In late 1967 Dr. Becker was contacted by Rexford Daniels, a consultant for a consortium of professional engineers and electronics companies that was preparing a report to advise the government regarding how to divide the spectrum of man-made electromagnetic energy among the various competing interests. In all the contemplated uses of the spectrum, the energy would pass through the environment to the aerial of a receiving device, necessarily impinging on human beings. Daniels had been charged to investigate the possibility of side-effects and he asked Dr. Becker to write a report about the issue.

In that report Dr. Becker said that there were definite biological effects due to man-made environmental electromagnetic energy and that the most important effects in humans occurred in the central nervous system. He said the seemingly logical expectation that the strongest effects would be associated with the highest levels was not supported by the literature, and that whether long-term exposures were cumulative was unknown. He recommended that the exact modes of interaction between electromagnetic energy and living organisms be determined as quickly as possible so that the possible hazards could be estimated with a much higher degree of certainty than was then possible. He concluded, "It should be emphasized that certain industrial or communication techniques could result in the exposure of relatively large population groups to energy fields entirely without the knowledge of the exposed individuals." But his report to Daniels was not distributed or mentioned in the final report by the consortium to the government, which said that side-effects of environmental electromagnetic energy "are being increasingly identified" and recommended only that a list of them be maintained, divided between those that are beneficial and those that are harmful.

In the context of public inquiries like the Daniels report, Dr. Becker suspected that when his advice about environmental hazards of electromagnetic energy was sought, the purpose was only to create an illusion that all aspects of the issue had been seriously considered. He was also consulted privately from time to time by various government agencies but always seemed skeptical regarding whether his advice had any impact. I don't think he ever saw any evidence that it had. He seemed to recognize that what he had to say about the potential dangers of electromagnetic energy was not being taken seriously. Nevertheless he continued to express his opinions in progressively stronger terms.

In June 1968 I received my PhD and Dr. Becker asked me to continue working in his laboratory. The offer was unexpected because I felt I had not been of any material assistance to him in the development and advancement of his ideas. I believed that the concept of doping atoms in nerves was probably erroneous, that the bone semiconductor theory was not necessarily the correct interpretation of his data, that the ability of natural currents in bone to orient molecules of the collagen protein during new bone formation was wrong, that the famous experiment he had done with Bassett showing that artificial DC currents made bone grow was a trivial result that had been published many times before he and Bassett performed their study, and that the link between man and his environment had nothing much to do with semiconduction. On the other hand, he had done some amazing experiments and had generated many exciting ideas that in my perspective, as limited as it was at that time, had the ring of truth and an enormous potential to help humanity. Most important of all was my respect and admiration for the man himself. He always was exactly as he appeared to be: gruff, but impeccably honest; stubborn, but intensely focused on what was important; prone to adopt the interpretation of his data that favored his theory without giving due consideration to alternative explanations, but brave to the point that he would suggest ideas and consider possibilities that frightened ordinary investigators into silence. I wanted nothing more than to please and help him, but I found that frustratingly difficult to do. I didn't think about the big picture the way he did, but then neither did anybody else I knew about. What I did think about was how to best sharpen, improve, and validate his vision. Unfortunately that wasn't what it seemed he wanted me to do. Not that he wanted me to pursue other goals; just that he didn't enthusiastically embrace what I thought I should be doing.

I didn't hesitate even a moment before I accepted his offer. I told him

I wanted to concentrate on the issue of whether piezoelectric charge in bone controlled its growth. He approved my plan, telling me that he was confident that any possible result would support his overall conception of an electrical growth-control system in the body.

After Friedman finished his rabbit study I went to his office to talk about it.

"Did the magnetic fields affect the brains of the rabbits?" I asked.

"Some had brain pathology that consisted of scattered areas of dead tissue."

"Are you saying that the magnetic field was responsible?"

"Yes and no. I saw dead areas in both exposed and control rabbits, but the effect was greater in the rabbits that were exposed to the field."

"What sense do you make of that?" I asked.

"It raises the question of a possible stress effect," he replied. " Laboratory rabbits have a parasite in their brains. Normally it does no damage because it is held in check by the body's defense mechanisms. The results of my experiment suggested a possible stress effect induced by the magnetic field that unmasked an otherwise routinely undetectable disease. Barnothy found similar effects in mice."

Madeleine Barnothy asked Dr. Becker to write a chapter on the biological effects of electromagnetic energy for a book she was editing. During a discussion of the papers he intended to include in his chapter, we began talking about the effects of electromagnetic energy on the brain and how they related to his growth-control system.

"There would appear to be little doubt that some interaction exists between brain function and weak external electromagnetic energy," he said.

"It's quite a big idea," I replied, "but it seems right."

"The concept has been viewed with considerable skepticism in scientific quarters because civilized man is exposed to a multitude of different kinds of electromagnetic energy, all apparently with no effect whatsoever. But there are effects. You just have to look with an open mind."

"Are you thinking about more than just the earth's magnetic field?" I asked.

"Much more than that. I'm thinking about our technology. It may well be productive of electromagnetic environments that have significant and potentially undesirable effects on the human population," he replied.

"What do you mean 'potentially undesirable'?"

"Some carefully controlled applications may be useful for promoting healing. But when the energy is just a kind of pollution, something unavoidable and involuntary for the public, it's hard to think of any effects that such energy produces as beneficial."

After a pause during which he took several puffs on his pipe he said, "If you take all the studies together they indicate the occurrence of an interaction between the energy and some active property of the brain that is acutely sensitive to such a modality, resulting in an overall effect on the function of the brain."

He took another puff and said, "We need to determine the basis for the interaction between neural structures and electromagnetic energy. Only with this knowledge can we intelligently predict the possible undesirable effects of human exposures. Such knowledge could also lead to testable hypotheses and possible therapeutic uses as well as increasing our knowledge of neural functioning itself."

"What is your idea about what the basis of the interaction might be?"

"I think that the DC voltages and currents of nerve tissue are the target. I believe that we can discount any possibility of the effect being primarily upon the action potential per se. The DC voltages display analog-type variations in response to certain basic stimuli and also are related in possibly a causal fashion to the efficiency of the action-potential system."

"Are you saying that the body has a special sense for detecting electromagnetic energy?"

"The DC voltages serve as a primitive analog data-transmitting and control system which regulates the ability of the brain to process data via the more sophisticated digital system based on action-potentials. It is interesting that some time ago, on a cybernetic basis, Von Neumann discussed the need for an analog-type of data transmission system in the brain that was additional to the action-potential system that it regulated. All animals that have even a rudimentary nervous system have a DC system, and in each case the pattern reflects the anatomy of the system."

"So you believe that the voltages produce currents and that somehow both of them are targets of the energy?"

"Yes. From a theoretical point of view, the existence of standing potentials in a conducting network implies a current flow sufficient to maintain the potential."

"But that's not true," I said, "if your idea of current is like what flows in a copper wire, which is what I understand you are saying. That current is made up of electrons flowing in a solid. The DC voltages you measured probably came from ions flowing in water. And to make matters even more complicated, currents in tissues are separated into different compartments by membranes that allow some kinds of ions to pass but not others. There might hundreds of these membranes in one inch of tissue. So relating the DC voltages in tissues to an electronic current may not be a good basis for explaining the brain's sensitivity to electromagnetic energy."

"You are neglecting the Hall effect study, which showed that the current flow is semiconducting in nature and involved the flow of electrons," he said.

"I don't know how to explain those results unless I repeat the experiment," I replied. "But I think perhaps it was a mistake to base the concept of a link between man and the environment on the results of that study. The link surely seems real but I am afraid you are backing the wrong explanation."

"My thesis is that the DC system exerts some regulatory effect upon the overall functioning of the brain and is acutely sensitive to applied electromagnetic energy. I proposed this thesis proposed primarily as a working hypothesis. It explains the majority of the reported phenomena and provides a testable hypothesis."

"Fine. But why not base the hypothesis of sensitivity to electromagnetic energy on a more biological theory, which is your turf, rather than a biophysical theory, which is the turf of the Shamoses of this world. They despise the way you use their terms and concepts and I think will never let you succeed. It's a fight you don't need and can't win."

"Something that emerged from Howard's studies might be what you are talking about," he said.

"What?" I asked.

"Stress," he replied.

"That sounds reasonable. I'd like to talk about that possibility. But here, I want to make the important point that we should focus on proving indisputably that there is a link, and pay less attention to the problem of explaining the underlying mechanism. If you succeed in proving the link between external energy and brain function, then logically there must be a physics-type explanation and it will be someone else's problem to find it. You'll need only a biological rationale, something that makes sense to biologists and clinicians. That's a far lower hurdle than the one you are attempting to clear now with the engineers."

He shrugged and walked away, leaving me with the feeling that he was not persuaded.

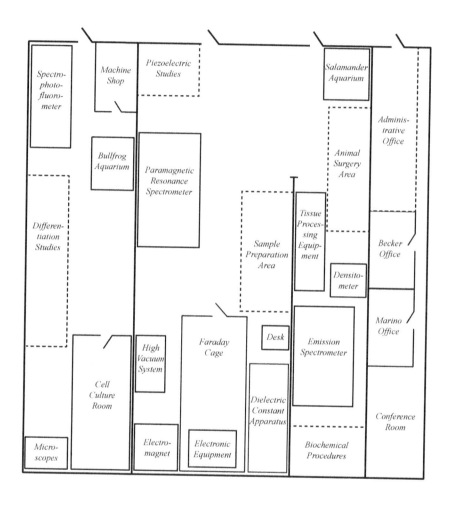

Dr. Becker's laboratory on the ninth floor of the Veterans Administration hospital in Syracuse, New York, in the 1960s.

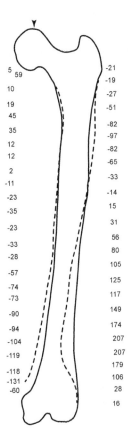

Outline of a human femur depicting the location and strength of measurements of surface charge that resulted when a simulated force comparable to that associated with walking was applied (arrow). The dotted femoral outline was the result under the assumption that the surface charge governed bone building and bone resorption. Published in "Piezoelectric Effect and Growth Control in Bone" in 1970.

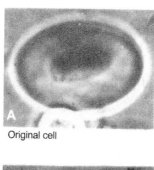

Original cell

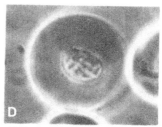

Cell rounded, nucleus changed

Initial changes, projections
from nucleus to cell membrane

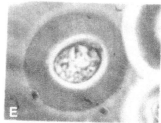

Cytoplasm more transparent,
further nuclear changes

Ring forms around nucleus,
cytoplasm more uniform

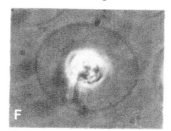

Final stage, cytoplasm almost
transparent

Frog red blood cell passing through changes due to stimulation by less than a thousand millionth of an ampere of DC current. The time interval between successive photomicrographs was about 3–6 minutes. The cell was photographed by Dr. Becker in 1969, at a magnification of 1200 times.

Chapter 8:

Summit

1970–1973: He pursues studies on bone healing, discovers that salamanders can regenerate a heart, produces partial limb regeneration in rats using electrical energy, confronts the problem of commercialization of electromagnetic medical devices, receives an NIH grant to study acupuncture, writes openly about the dangers of man-made electromagnetic energy in the environment, and becomes recognized as pre-eminent in the field

For more than a decade Dr. Becker had steadfastly pursued the idea that growth and healing were emergent phenomena controlled by electromagnetic signals that occurred naturally within the body. He published papers, obtained grants, spoke at many scientific meetings, and built a productive research laboratory. Even so, his foremost responsibility always was to practice medicine and manage a busy clinical service. His clinical workload increased steadily because of patients injured in the Vietnam War who needed reconstructive surgery or labor-intensive bedside care for bone infections. He had no protected time for his nonclinical duties, so he attended to them only after his daily clinical obligations had been met.

You might think that the constant clinical pressure would have sapped his energy for research or at least dulled his ability to see the larger picture and make appropriate plans, but the opposite occurred. His clinical experience energized him, constantly reminding him of the need to pursue the path he was following. Unlike the "establishment," his term for academic biologists, he viewed research as an ethical responsibility and chose his objectives carefully in the hope of accomplishing something meaningful for human beings.

As chief of the research service, he attempted to reform the research practices at the hospital and to assist those on the expanding clinical staff who sought his help in starting research programs. But for every two problems he solved three new ones appeared. The hospital administrators did not see research as beneficial to the health of veterans and frequently were uncooperative regarding even routine management issues involving research, although usually not to the extent that might trigger intervention by officials at Central Office. They held Dr. Becker in high regard and used the research service in Syracuse as a model for other hospitals, sending new research chiefs to Syracuse for training. Central Office ended that program after a new chief from the Buffalo VA complained that Dr. Becker had ignored her during her time in Syracuse. He was concerned that he had apparently disappointed his benefactors in Central Office, but told me, "There aren't enough hours in the day to please everyone."

He knew that DC currents appeared naturally at injury sites in animals and human beings. In frogs, according to his research, when the injury was a broken bone, the currents caused red blood cells to de-differentiate, thereby providing the stem cells that re-differentiated into osteoblasts, the cells that built the reparative bone. But when the injury was an amputation, the stem cells never re-differentiated to form a new limb. I asked him why he continued to devote so much attention to frogs and de-differentiation, considering that few experimental biologists seemed to care about frogs, and among those who did, there was great hostility toward his ideas.

"Because understanding de-differentiation is the only path by which human beings will be able to regenerate organs and limbs," he replied. "We must learn how it occurs so that it can be stimulated to take place in humans."

"Why is de-differentiation the only path?" I asked.

"Everyone who ever studied regeneration in salamanders saw that a mass of stem cells formed at the cut end of the leg and then turned into all the kinds of cells that were necessary for a new limb."

"Where do the stem cells come from?" I asked.

"According to dogma they migrate from other parts of the body."

"You don't think that's true?"

"I'm certain it's not true, despite what the establishment says."

"Where do you think the cells come from?"

"They are manufactured by de-differentiation. Electrical signals turn red blood cells back into stem cells."

"The same as in frogs?" I asked.

"Yes and no. The electrical signals at injury sites can de-differentiate the red blood cells, but the signals aren't able to trigger re-differentiation into all the different tissues needed for a new limb, so frogs normally don't regrow a new limb. But they could if the cells got the right signal."

"How do you know that?"

"Because a biologist at the University of Kentucky did it a few years ago."

"You mean he cut off a limb in a frog and then supplied an additional electrical signal, and the frog grew a new limb?"

"That's exactly what I mean," he replied.

"Do people de-differentiate?"

"No, but I think they could under the right circumstances."

"But people can heal," I said. "If the skin is cut, new skin grows. If a bone is broken, new bone grows."

"Skin and bone healing are just the tip of the iceberg of what is possible. They are simple kinds of healing that don't involve stem cells, only local dormant cells of the type already recognizable as skin cells, bone cells, or muscle cells; the dormant cells are activated by electrical signals caused by the injury."

"What's the difference between a dormant cell and a stem cell?"

"A stem cell is like a God cell, it can do anything. It has all the power of the first cell of the organism, the original fertilized egg. We need to discover the nature of the signal that could trigger stem cells to form in human beings."

"Is that really possible?"

"Why not? The only reason it hasn't been discovered is the dogmatic commandment that 'Thou shalt not study de-differentiation.' The biological establishment demands that the process of repressing DNA to make specific types of mature cells be considered irreversible. De-differentiation is heresy."

"That attitude makes no sense," I said. "It turns the idea of science upside down."

"It would make sense if you knew more about how dogma works in biology. De-differentiation goes against the idea that living organisms are only simple machines that can't dynamically regulate their own activities."

He had previously discovered the surprising fact that frog red blood cells suspended in a salt solution in a dish could be de-differentiated by exceedingly weak electrical signals, and that signals only slightly stronger simply did not work. He hypothesized that the same process produced the stem cells responsible for limb regeneration in salamanders and began experiments to test the theory. His technician, Sharon Chapin, anesthetized a salamander, opened the chest cavity, cut the heart in half to allow the cavity to fill with blood, recovered the red cells, and suspended them in a salt solution. For months Dr. Becker passed ultraweak electrical currents through the cell suspensions while viewing them under a microscope, as he had done in his earlier studies of frog cells, but found no evidence that the salamander cells had reverted to stem cells. He remained convinced that his theory was correct but nevertheless turned his attention to other kinds of experiments. I thought that decision was unwise because the evidence he sought was important to support his story. I mentioned my concern and proposed that he consider variants of the procedure he had followed, but he told me sharply, "I'm moving on."

Chapin didn't immediately get the message to terminate the cell-prep-aration procedures so she continued to perform them. But rather than disposing of the salamanders after having collected the cells, she simply closed the chest incision with stiches and returned the salamanders to the aquarium. Two days later she was surprised to see them swimming more or less normally. Dr. Becker studied some injured animals and saw that the blood flow ceased immediately after the heart was cut but resumed about five hours later. When he examined microscope slides of the hearts he was astonished to see that the part of the heart that had been cut away had regenerated. He also saw that cells at the injury site were identical to the stem cells he had seen in the frogs, which suggested to him that the new muscle cells had been produced by the processes of de-differentiation and re-differentiation.

The fortuitous observation of heart regeneration pleased him even though it didn't directly support his electrical theories because he had made no electrical measurements, and thus had no evidence that could permit him to argue that electrical signals were the trigger that brought about the de-differentiation. Nevertheless he was the first to report that salamanders could grow a new heart, which he did in *Nature*, continuing his unprec-edented string of publications in that prestigious journal.

I had been doing experiments involving piezoelectricity in an effort to understand its role in bone growth, but became progressively more in-terested in the aspect of Dr. Becker's work that involved the interaction of applied electromagnetic energy and living systems. I decided I wanted to concentrate my research in that area and put forward a plan to directly test his idea that cells and animals were affected by electromagnetic energy. He was pleased with what I proposed and readily approved the initial studies I described. Soon after I began the studies I encountered the argument that there were no known mechanisms by which the energy could act on a living system, and that the proper course of experimentation involved the evaluation of hypotheses regarding possible mechanisms of interaction. But I saw the primary question as whether there were reproducible effects. The scientific method permitted a resolution of that question irrespective of any knowledge regarding the mechanisms. I thought it would be foolish to conduct experiments to validate particular mechanisms without first establishing that effects actually existed, because nonexistent effects have no mechanisms. I quickly realized that my perspective was in the distinct minority, and that I was entering a controversial area in which defending the research required strong arguments as well as good experimental data. I decided I wanted to attend law school and asked Dr. Becker to adjust my official work schedule at the hospital so that I could do so. He asked why I wanted to go to law school and I told him I thought that the training would help me to learn how to explain and defend our work. I never knew whether he accepted my rationale but he agreed to my request.

Early in his research Dr Becker had suggested that if the DC voltages at an amputation site in a frog were modified by means of the application of an external electromagnetic signal similar to the one that occurs at the amputation stump of a salamander, then frogs might also be able to regenerate limbs. Even if he had wanted to test that idea experimentally, however, he had no knowledge of how to make an implantable device that could mimic the temporally changing DC voltages in salamanders that had lost a limb. But in 1967 an anatomist at the University of Kentucky named Stephen Smith had devised a primitive version of such a device and implanted them in the amputation stumps of frogs. When he sacrificed the animals three months later and examined the tissues under a microscope he found clear evidence that the regeneration process had been started, a result consistent with Dr. Becker's theory.

At a lab meeting he surprised us when he said he intended to use Smith-type devices to try to induce regeneration in the rat, a mammal. We all knew he had no fear of criticism, but even by his standards the proposed experiment was audacious. Nevertheless he had the will and the necessary resources to take that step, and no one in the room doubted that was exactly what he would do.

The task of building the devices fell to Joe Spadaro, who had recently completed his PhD and had begun to focus his research in the area of bioelectrochemistry. He made devices that consisted of two thin metal wires joined end to end, one of silver and one of platinum. The dissimilarity of the metals spontaneously created a DC voltage between the free ends of the wires, silver negative and platinum positive. The device was an exceedingly crude simulation of the dynamic electrical changes that occurred naturally at an injury site. On the other hand, bench-top measurements showed that the current it produced was reasonably comparable to that naturally present in the body.

Dr. Becker amputated one of the front limbs in a series of young rats and implanted a device in each amputation site. Amazingly, the microscope slides showed that some limb regeneration occurred in most of the animals within only a few days of the injury. Except for Dr. Becker, no one in the laboratory expected that result. I doubted there was an experimental biologist in any university who would have expected it.

He submitted a report of the study for publication and was distressed by the sarcasm and antagonism of some of the anonymous reviewers. He had been asked many times by journal editors to review papers, and his comments regarding them were always shaped by his beliefs that the reviewer's job was to help the authors improve their work, and that the tone of the review should always be polite and civil. "If you wouldn't say it to the author's face, don't misuse your anonymity and say it in the review," was the advice he gave me the first time I was asked to review a paper. Some of his reviewers, however, did not follow those rules. One reviewer conceded there were no obvious shortcomings in the report but advised against publication "because the results were not important." Dr. Becker replied that the comment "was not helpful in improving my work." The same reviewer wrote, "It is not so easy to grow new limbs," seemingly suggesting that he thought Dr. Becker believed otherwise. He responded, "I know." To the comment, "Even currents that are strong enough to cause shock apparently don't grow new limbs," he responded, "The comment was not relevant to my work." Another reviewer didn't believe the results because "no one else had reported regeneration caused by very weak stimuli." Dr. Becker answered, "I respectfully disagree with this logic." To the reviewer who told him to repeat the entire experiment "to make sure that the results were repeatable," Dr. Becker responded, "My granting agency does not allow me to do the same experiment more than once." Another reviewer objected to publication of the study because the rats hadn't grown a complete new limb. Dr. Becker told him that his "expectations were unrealistic," and in a note to the editor wrote, "He wouldn't be satisfied unless the rats could play the piano." The comment that angered Dr. Becker the most came from a reviewer who did not believe that Dr. Becker had actually observed what he reported, but rather had fabricated the data. The reviewer called Dr. Becker's report "plain ordinary fraud."

A common criticism in the reviews related to the cause of the new growth. Dr. Becker thought that the electrical signal from the device was indisputably responsible, although other explanations were theoretically possible, as always. I showed him a list of alternative explanations with arguments against them, straw men intended to formally recognize that the possibilities were unlikely, a conventional trope in scientific writing. But he forcefully dismissed my suggested strategy. "I don't follow their rules. He said. "If they believe any of that crap they should do the experiment and publish their results."

To satisfy the general concerns of the editor Dr. Becker agreed to the humiliating requirement that independent experts be allowed to examine his microscope slides. Lent Johnson, chief of pathology at the Armed Forces Institute of Pathology, and Marcus Singer, an anatomy professor at Case Western Reserve University, visited the laboratory and examined the slides, and both attested to the veracity of Dr. Becker's results, which were ultimately published in several journals, including *Nature*.

Late in 1971, Carl Brighton, an up-and-coming orthopedic surgeon at the University of Pennsylvania, finally took the step that Dr. Becker and Bassett had long declined to take, each for his own reason—the use of man-made electrical energy to treat a patient who had a bone disorder. Brighton's patient was a woman with an unhealed ankle fracture, a "nonunion," and he decided to apply electrical energy, hoping it would make bone grow as Dr. Becker and Bassett had found seven years earlier in dogs. Brighton drilled a steel pin into her ankle at the site of the nonunion and connected the pin to the negative terminal of a battery. He avoided the undesirable bone resorption that had occurred at the positive terminal in the dog study by connecting his positive terminal to a large metal plate placed on the patient's skin. After three months of continuous electrical treatment, the bone began to heal. Although the result appeared to generally support Dr. Becker's theories, in actuality that was not the case, at least that's what I thought, and I mentioned my concerns to him:

"Do you really think that what Brighton did is good for us, I mean that it actually supports your idea that growth and healing are controlled by natural electromagnetic energy?" I asked.

"You don't?" he replied.

"Well I wonder about it. Suppose your theory is correct. Then of course there must be a reason, a physical process that connects energy and healing. Further, we know that energy from a battery can grow bone. The dog study showed that. So there must also be a reason why that happened. If the two reasons were completely different, neither of the two battery studies, dog or human, would support your theory."

He puffed on his pipe and replied, "I think that the two reasons are the same."

"That's difficult to accept, " I said. "The energy level of the current that the battery produced in tissues, although tiny compared with the current in an electrical motor or a light bulb, was a million times higher than natural currents in the body. Do you really want to take the position that X and a million times X both do the same thing in the body by means of the same mechanism?"

"Where do you get your numbers from for the level of the natural signals in the body?" he asked.

"From your measurements of DC voltages and Ohm's law, which makes the values easy to compute, from our piezoelectric studies, and from your rat regeneration study."

"Do you know the reasons that Brighton's currents made bone grow?" he asked.

"I think I do," I replied. He motioned for me to continue so I said, "Electrical energy from the battery was converted into chemical energy at the negative electrode in the patient's foot, resulting in increased pH and the formation of various electrochemicals. They acted as poisons that inflamed the tissues, and the inflammatory response activated dormant bone cells."

"What electrochemicals are you talking about?"

"I don't know exactly. But whatever they were, they were undoubtedly there, produced by the combination of high pH and iron atoms that dissolved from the pin. I think no one doubts that."

"Then according to you these chemicals made bone cells build bone?"

"Yes. You could make the chemical brew in a beaker, inject it into a patient, and it would grow bone. You know that there are reports of animal studies where exactly that occurred. Actually any form of energy makes bone grow, not just energy from a battery. There are experiments in which bone grew in response to pressure, tapping with a hammer, dripping acid on the bone, applying a heated rod, implanting a rusty nail, or injecting toxic chemicals. Every one of these things inflamed the tissues and resulted in bone growth. It seems that growing bone is easy. There's nothing special about electromagnetic energy."

"How could all those different stimuli have the same effect?" he asked.

"I don't have any detailed explanation, but it is what it is. There just isn't any doubt about the fact that the response of the bone cells is nonspecific in the sense that any form of energy can trigger them. The only requirements are that the strength of the stimulus be above a minimum threshold but below an acutely toxic level. Brighton knew exactly what the optimal level for electricity was because of your dog study."

"You make it seem as if the dog study and what Brighton did had no relation to electromagnetic energy, and that the bone growth was a purely chemical effect," he said.

"Exactly" I replied. "That's why I think his report is not evidence in support of your theory, despite appearances to the contrary. Your theory is completely different. It operates at a tremendously smaller level of energy and is based on direct information supplied by the brain. That's what you have always said, at least that's what I understood."

"You are missing something important about the dog study," he said. "It came about as a result of prior studies that led to a prediction that bone would grow at the negative electrode. When a prediction based on a theory is substantiated, how can you say that the result is not support for the theory? Elementary principles of science say the opposite."

"I agree that it *looks like* support, but the matter doesn't end there. One must go further and determine whether there is another theory that better explains the results. That's what Brighton did. According to him, his result has nothing to do with your theory. He thinks your theory is ridiculous."

"Why do you say that?"

"Because I have friends in the bioengineering department at Penn who work with him, and that's what they told me. His story is that changes in oxygen levels triggered by inflammation stimulated the dormant bone cells."

"That's nonsense," he said.

"I'm not saying his story is right," I replied, "only that your dog study can have other explanations, so it doesn't necessarily support your theory."

"So my results occurred by chance?" he asked rhetorically.

"No. They occurred as a result of electrochemical laws and the natural reactive properties of tissues and bone cells. But they probably have no relation to your theory even though on the surface they seem to support your theory."

"I think you are emphasizing mechanistic issues too much," he said. "That is not what is primarily important."

"What is?" I asked.

"First, the validity of the experimental result, whether what seemed to happen actually happened. Second, the utility of the result. Research should have a practical ultimate purpose. It's not a game for personal amusement. Mechanisms are third in importance. They can serve as a storyboard so that people who don't have time or inclination to look at the details can feel satisfied that the result isn't phony, like something you might see at a carnival sideshow. Any physician who does an experiment must have a storyboard so that he won't be attacked by the biology establishment."

"I think we can agree that Brighton's result had utility."

"Just because the nonunion healed?" he asked.

"Yes."

"Well let's suppose that my theory is correct, as you proposed a few minutes ago, and also that your electrochemical theory is responsible for the bone that grew in the patient."

"Yes."

"Then Brighton's result had no clinical utility. And worse, it is potentially dangerous."

"Why do you say that?"

"He is applying energy of the type that the body normally uses to regulate its growth, but he is slamming the patient with levels of that energy that far exceed the natural levels. Who can say what the result might be. Cancer perhaps?"

"Well I suppose that's a possibility any time someone tries a new clinical method of treatment," I replied.

"That's why the side effects should be studied in animals before experiments are done on people," he said.

"That sounds reasonable. Do you think that Brighton didn't do that?"

"I know for a fact that he didn't. He just suggested the treatment to the patient. She agreed because patients always do what their doctor suggests. It was an interesting clinical experiment but the sad thing is that he took unnecessary risks."

"What do you mean?" I asked.

"A standard treatment for a nonunion is a bone graft. It's a minor operation that takes less than an hour and is 85% successful. Brighton replaced that treatment with one that required the patient to undergo an operation to place the steel pin in her bone. Then she had to walk around for three months with the electrode connected to a battery by means of a wire that passed through her skin to the battery, which she had to change every day. The wire was a path to the bone for infection. Infected bone is a nasty disease. Then, after another operation to remove the pin, she had to wear a cast for three months. What Brighton did is nonsensical from practical and risk-benefit points of view."

"I didn't think about that," I said.

"There are other things you didn't think about," he replied, and before I could even ask him what he meant he said, "We are on the edge of something important, something that can revolutionize clinical medicine. The old dogmas are being challenged and their grip on the minds of clinicians is starting to slip. The grants that I get, the ones that pay all the salaries here, are proof of that. But there is a lot of basic work that needs to be done, pioneering work. If the settlers move in now, that could restrict our progress, even end it."

"What kind of settlers are you thinking of?" I asked.

"People who want to commercialize bioelectricity, not explore for its safest and best use," he replied.

"Wouldn't commercialization be a good thing because it would bring publicity and interest in the area?"

"It would have the opposite effect. Companies will arrest progress. I've seen it happen. From their perspective they have the final answers, and they are interested only in selling their particular devices. They make only baby-step improvements or no improvements at all, things like changing the color of the packaging or creating new advertisements."

"Do you really think that companies will get involved?" I asked. "Brighton has treated only one patient."

"He has done much more," he replied. "He applied for a patent, and started a company."

We were interrupted by one of the hospital carpenters who wanted to see Dr. Becker about recurrent pains he was having in his lower back, so I left the room while they talked and then returned when I saw the carpenter depart. When we resumed our conversation I inquired further into his attitude about mechanisms.

"On one hand," I said, "you give the question of mechanisms low priority, but on the other hand you never miss an opportunity to talk about them."

"Did you ever hear the story about the donkey and the two-by-four?" he asked.

"I don't think so," I replied.

"A farmer who was training his donkey invited a neighbor to watch. The first thing the farmer did was to pick up a two-by-four and wallop the donkey on its head. As it struggled to get back on its feet the shocked neighbor asked how that would help train the donkey, and the farmer replied, 'That wasn't for training, it was to get his attention.' That's what stories about mechanisms do, they pacify the academic biologists, who are the people that the granting agencies use to decide who should get money, and how much. The establishment regards the stories as the hallmark of science and recommends providing funds only after they perceive a credible story. Without stories this laboratory would not exist."

Central Office notified Dr. Becker that his application for the position of Medical Investigator was approved, which meant that he could devote up to 75% of his time to research. One of his first steps was to pursue his interest in acupuncture, which he had come to suspect might be related to his ideas concerning the flow of information in the nervous system. He invited an acupuncturist to make a clinical presentation at orthopedics grand rounds. The chief of the medical staff strongly opposed Dr. Becker's plan but he told me, "I am going to do it, and I don't care what he thinks. There is nothing he can say or do that will stop me."

The patient selected for presentation suffered from severe degenerative osteoarthritis in his knee. During the grand rounds the acupuncturist inserted more than a dozen needles into the patient, not only in the vicinity of his knee, but also in the web between his thumb and index finger and in his earlobes. From time to time and not according to any particular pattern that I could discern, the acupuncturist returned to one of the inserted needles and adjusted it slightly, either twirling it or moving it up and down. After about fifteen minutes from the time he had begun the treatment, the patient's knee could be moved through a greatly increased range of motion without causing any pain. He cried with joy, the audience clapped loudly, and Dr. Becker smiled one of his ultra-rare smiles.

Acupuncturists had envisioned some vaguely characterized form of energy flowing throughout the body along pathways that had been defined in antiquity but were invisible by modern imaging methods. Dr. Becker believed that acupuncture was actually a control system mediated by the flow of electromagnetic energy that was altered by the insertion of needles, thereby producing relief from pain. He applied for an NIH grant to pursue his ideas and his application was funded. He hired Maria Reichmanis to do the work; she became the third PhD in physics on his staff.

From the beginning of his research Dr. Becker addressed questions that were ignored by the famous experimental biologists, questions that could be considered only by means of a holistic approach to experimentation. His efforts led him to discover an electrical control system based on the flow of natural electromagnetic energy. It was a unique scientific insight with far-reaching implications, regardless of whether the system was mediated by semiconductivity, as he believed, or by some other process. One logical implication was that electromagnetic energy produced by a man-made device might be employed for therapeutic purposes, perhaps to treat disabilities or cure disease. The task, as he saw it, was to discover the natural control signal that was associated with the maintenance of healthy tissue and then to mimic that signal artificially with the aim of restoring health after disease had occurred. He focused on the kinds of clinical problems he typically treated, and fleshed out his ideas in several talks and publications in which he suggested that orthopedic surgery had taken the wrong turn by employing metal and plastic implants as replacements for damaged hip and knee joints. He argued that implants decline in strength continuously from the moment they are placed in the body, and that it would be far better to attempt to grow new joints. He pointed to his de-differentiation and limb-regeneration studies as support for the plausibility of his suggestion.

Another implication of his theory was that man-made electromagnetic energy could inadvertently cause disease. This was the area where his work came into conflict with that of Bassett and Brighton. Dr. Becker believed they were proceeding with undue haste, motivated mostly by economic considerations, and without sufficient safeguards to protect the patients from unevaluated risks. In his publications and during conversations with Bassett and Brighton he told them he thought there was danger in "tinkering with the body's language" without first studying the potential consequences and identifying the medical conditions where the risk/benefit ratio clearly justified the electromagnetic intervention. They both took great umbrage each time he made these points. More than one orthopedist who was friendly to Dr. Becker warned against antagonizing such powerful and respected members of the orthopedic establishment, but he ignored the advice and encouraged me to continue my studies of the effects of applied electromagnetic energy.

I began experiments to see if anything would happen to animals treated with energy at intensity levels comparable to those employed in medical devices that were under investigation at various locations in the US and abroad. My initial results stunned both of us. Some exposed rats developed strange swollen eyes. Exposed mice died more frequently than the controls and the survivors failed to thrive. Dr. Becker sent photographers to the animal-care facility to take pictures of the affected animals. The endpoints I had measured were chosen arbitrarily rather than because we had a basis to predict that they were particularly likely to be affected. The implication therefore was that electromagnetic energy was capable of producing a broad range of physiological effects, an implication that seemed reliable even though I had no knowledge of the mechanism of interaction between the animals and the energy.

In a magazine article published late in 1972, Dr. Becker forcefully described his perspective regarding the biological effects of electromagnetic energy. I spoke with him several weeks after I had read it.

"What made you decide to write the article?"

"In March I gave a talk at a convention of engineers in New York. The editor of MIT's *Technology Review* was there and asked me to write an article about what I said."

"What did you talk about?" I asked.

"My point was that various biological effects due to electromagnetic energy had been reported but engineers were reluctant to recognize them as valid because their thinking didn't provide a mechanism. I described my work to support the thesis that organisms possess semiconducting properties at the cellular and tissue level, and that this was the level where electromagnetic energy interacted with living organisms, so there was a mechanism."

"You seem to have gone further in the article," I said.

"I warned about unintended consequences of the energy. Engineers are building ever more powerful antennas as well as little black boxes that make different kinds of electromagnetic energy, and doctors have started using to treat diseases. There are possible dangers in the indiscriminate addition of man-made electromagnetic energy into the environment, and in the premature acceptance of electromagnetic energy as a therapeutic modality."

In the most low-key tone and manner that I was capable of, hoping I would not give offense but rather would be appreciated for my honesty and good intentions, I said, "I think there is a fundamental problem with your argument in favor of a mechanistic role for semiconduction."

"What do you mean?" he answered curtly.

"You said you had shown that electromagnetic energy can change fundamental life processes in animals and man by perturbing the electronic control systems that regulate basic life functions."

"Yes."

"But electronic conduction processes obey linear laws, and all of the biological phenomena you referred to obey nonlinear laws."

"I don't know what you mean," he said.

"In the article you wrote, 'We were able to study some of the electrical parameters of importance; the most outstanding was that the effective levels of voltage and current had both upper and lower limits.' In other words, you said that voltages or currents above some upper limit were nonproductive of cellular changes, at least until the currents became so high that heating occurs."

"Yes, I said that because a little energy made the cells change but more energy didn't make them change faster. Instead, the cells didn't change at all," he explained.

"That means the changes had to have been governed by nonlinear laws, not semiconduction," I said. "Only a nonlinear law would allow no change when you increased the energy. Linear laws, in contrast, always predict a bigger effect when the stimulus is stronger."

"Is all this your idea?" he asked.

"No. It began with the recent theoretical advancements in studying the weather"

"Weather?"

"A certain combination of thermal, chemical, and mechanical energy in the atmosphere might lead to a prediction of rain. But if the thermal energy were increased, less rain or even no rain at all might be predicted. In nonlinear systems, cause and effect are not directly proportional and one can become the other. Nobody knew that nonlinear systems were anything more than mathematical abstractions until the discovery that the weather was just such a system."

"So you are saying that the body's reaction to electromagnetic energy is another example?"

"Exactly," I said. "You proved that."

"Couldn't reactions be linear sometimes and nonlinear at other times?"

"Perhaps, but what you are saying about the effects of electromagnetic energy would be more plausible if you were less forceful in trying to justify your position on the narrow basis of semiconduction because it is a strictly linear phenomenon. I'm talking about clinical applications and especially about your comments concerning the possible dangers of environmental electromagnetic energy."

"What comments?"

"You wrote, 'I also feel concern for a much broader problem, which is the continuous exposure of the entire North American population to an electromagnetic environment in which is present the possibility of inducing currents or voltages comparable with those now known to exist in biological control systems.'"

"What is your point?"

"Engineers argue that the electromagnetic environment is too weak to cause any effects. But their argument presumes that any effect the energy could cause must come about by means of linear laws, whereas your work clearly shows that the governing laws are nonlinear. One of the most interesting properties of nonlinear laws is that they can predict a significant response even from very small stimuli. So the argument of the engineers fails if you follow the lesson of your own experiments to its logical conclusion."

"Perhaps," he said, paused, and then continued as he left the room, "We'll see."

In September 1973, the New York Academy of Sciences sponsored the first international conference on electromagnetically mediated growth and healing, a field that Dr. Becker had essentially invented. Details of ongoing research in his laboratory that involved the effects of electromagnetic energy on wound healing, cartilage regeneration, infection control, and side-effects were presented in talks by his staff. He delivered the keynote lecture.

He began his lecture by pointing to the spectrum of interactions between electromagnetic energy and living organisms that he and others had reported, which he summarized as effects on levels of consciousness, spatial orientation, biorhythms, growth, and healing. He said that a theoretical mechanistic framework for the phenomena was needed, but that he would address an even more important issue, an explanation for why the effects occurred. He asked the audience to imagine, starting from lifeless material, how one might go about building an object that was alive and could react to electromagnetic energy in the manner demonstrated in reported experiments. He argued that reflection revealed such an object could not be endowed with all the properties of living systems simultaneously because the nervous system, for example, could not have developed until *after* life had been created. But even though the first living object could not have had a nervous system, it must have had some kind of primitive capability to modify its behavior in response to environmental factors, to self-organize and thereby survive. He said that in the absence of such a capability we could not regard the object as "alive."

How could the object be endowed with this primitive capability? One possibility, based on biochemistry, postulates the development of complex molecules in an aqueous solution, and their subsequent sequestration from the environment by some kind of membrane. But a better explanation, he said, derived from the concepts of the biological solid state, proposes an origin in crystalline structures that possess such properties as semiconductivity, photoconductivity, and piezoelectricity, all of which operate by means of a flow of electrons. A solid-state origin of life was far more likely to have occurred in response to natural forces, compared with a solution-chemistry origin wherein one is forced to assume that proteins, DNA, and cell membranes all developed simultaneously and spontaneously. He thus arrived at the idea that the proto-cell, the original living thing, must have been some kind of a self-organizing solid-state object.

Then by means of solution-based chemical reactions, evolution produced continuously increasing complexity. However, the original solid-state electronic control system was not eliminated, but rather became commingled with the water-based regulatory system. Thinking this way he concluded that there were two communications systems in the body. The later-developing water-based nervous system was digital, high-speed, and mediated information-intense functions such as thinking and somatic sensation. The earlier solid-based system was anatomically linked to the nervous system, but was analog, low-speed, and mediated the functions that he had studied, consciousness, orientation, biological rhythms, growth, and healing. He concluded his speech by saying that because of the way the digital system was constructed, it was relatively immune from the effects of man-made electromagnetic energy. But not so for the more primitive analog system, which he said could be affected for good or evil by such energy, depending on the circumstances. When he finished his talk almost everyone in the audience stood up and a long sustained applause ensued, one that the moderator of the session could not curtail despite his incessant thumping on the microphone, during which Dr. Becker smiled and nodded.

The next speaker was Andrew Bassett. He prefaced his talk by saying, "Ladies and gentlemen, we have just heard one of the most important talks in biology ever given." Then he focused on his topic and began listing the problems he had faced in his earlier dog experiments. In those studies bone formation was limited to discrete regions around the negative electrode, and electrode corrosion resulted in deleterious effects at both electrodes. Even more seriously, that method for applying electromagnetic energy required the use of transcutaneous wires, which could lead to bone infection. It therefore seemed advisable, he said, that the electromagnetic energy should be applied to the fracture site without the use of electrodes or wires. He said he had done that in a study involving dogs, the details of which would soon appear in *Science*. He expressed his intention to use the method clinically, saying that it could result in a 50% reduction in the time it took a fracture to heal. At this point he paused and said, "Fear has been expressed by some investigators in this area that electrical stimulation may result in cancer. No evidence of such effects was present in my experiments."

When Brighton gave his talk he said that a negative electrode could make bone grow, and he discounted any potential problems involving infection due to the wires, saying that had never occurred in any of his patients. He described evidence from rabbit studies that changes in oxygen levels occurred near the electrode, which he said was the reason bone grew at that location. He listed the optimal electrical conditions for altering the oxygen level, which were about the same as those Bassett had used in his first dog study. Brighton had begun using his method on humans who had sustained fractures that had not healed within the expected time. Using X-rays, he documented his latest successes, which were achieved in a 13-year-old boy and a 50-year-old woman.

The banquet for the conference was held in the main hall of the Academy headquarters. The three orthopedic surgeons sat at one of the large circular tables, each with a PhD from his staff seated to his immediate left, I beside Dr. Becker, Jonathan Black beside Brighton, and Arthur Pilla beside Bassett. Soon after we took our places, a glassy-eyed man approached our table, circled it slowly as if to identify each of the prominent speakers who sat there talking to one another, oblivious to his presence, at least until he stopped behind Dr. Becker and bent over so closely that there wasn't the width of two fingers between Dr. Becker's left ear and the intruder's nose. The name badge he wore identified him as Professor Lionel Jaffe from Purdue. He squinted at Dr. Becker and said, "You know nothing about science." Then he stood up straight, took a deep breath, bent over again, and said, "Your work is plain ordinary fraud." He then stumbled away and took a seat at a table in the back of the hall where I saw another man pat him on the back and shake his hand.

"Not one of your fans, I suppose," Bassett said. After the laughter died down he told Dr. Becker that the breadth of his perspective on biology and medicine was impressive, except for one point.

"You have said that the electromagnetic energy we are applying to our patients might cause cancer. But there is no evidence of that. Your fear is unwarranted and will likely be an incubus on progress in this field."

"By progress," Dr. Becker replied, "do you mean commercial progress?"

"I do," Bassett said, "but more. Electrotherapy may revolutionize medicine. If it can grow bone, why not cartilage and joints, or nerves? I think that in 20 years electrotherapy will be a standard tool in the armamentarium of the physician."

"You may be right, but you may also be wrong," replied Dr. Becker. "People will likely think that if Columbia University and the University of Pennsylvania say that the method is safe, then it must be safe. They will know nothing of the thinking that created the method, but their eyes will be glazed over by your promises."

The taciturn Brighton finally spoke, saying, "Scientific medicine proceeds step by step, by evolution not by revolution. Oxygen is the key to life. It is not surprising that electricity, which affects oxygen, should also affect growth."

"It is only a tool, not a panacea," said Black, and Brighton nodded approvingly.

"Are you saying that oxygen causes cancer?" the sarcastic Black said to Dr. Becker who returned a disdainful look.

At this point the voluble Pilla exclaimed, "Our method has nothing whatever to do with oxygen levels. Our method sends specific messages to particular kinds of cells telling the cells what to do."

"So your message to bone cells will be to build bone but not to cause cancer," Dr. Becker asked, and Pilla replied, "Exactly," oblivious to Dr. Becker's irony.

He had told me several times that, generally, he liked Pilla's thinking because it came from the perspective of communicating directly with cells, which could happen only if electromagnetic energy were the language of cells. However, Dr. Becker did not like Pilla's plans for a headlong rush toward commercialization.

He said to Pilla, "The basic principle is that electrical signals control the activity of cells. This capability can be exploited for therapeutic purposes, but it would be foolish to ignore the possibility that it could also cause disease. How can you be sure that you are always sending a beneficial message?"

"Nothing is perfect," said Bassett. "As physicians, we must always balance the risks against the benefits."

"On that we can agree," said Dr. Becker. "But is the risk of cancer worth the benefit of mobilizing a fracture patient one or two weeks earlier?"

"Bob, there is no risk whatsoever of cancer," said Bassett. "You invented it. You have no evidence. On the other hand the benefits are enormous. Millions of dollars would be saved and people would be returned to work sooner than would be expected."

"I agree with that," said Brighton.

Dr. Becker looked at Bassett, then Brighton, and then back to Bassett and said, "You both have your companies, and your patents. Are you speaking now as physicians or businessmen?"

"Bob, you sound like a spent force, afraid of the future that you helped create. Electrotherapy is coming, even if it is not perfect," Bassett replied.

Just before the dinner ended a Navy captain named Paul Tyler approached Dr. Becker and whispered, "We would like to request your help again on an important matter." Dr. Becker nodded and the two men agreed to speak later that evening. When they did, Tyler invited Dr. Becker to attend a meeting in Washington, DC, to review animal and human studies undertaken by the Navy that involved the biological effects of electromagnetic energy, and he accepted.

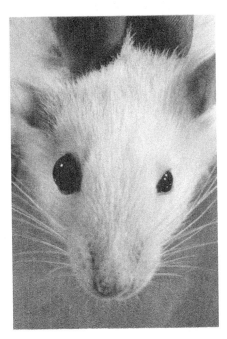

Rat exposed to electromagnetic energy for thirty days. Photographed in 1972.

Two litters of mice. The litter on the left was exposed to electromagnetic energy continuously from conception to maturity. A control litter (no exposure to the energy) is shown to the right. Photographed in 1973.

Chapter 9:

Turning

1974–1975: He learns about classified government research whose results support his theory about side-effects, loses an NIH grant, and submits written public testimony regarding his warning that man-made electromagnetic energy in the environment is a possible health risk

One morning in early January 1974 Dr. Becker told me his committee meeting in Washington had been "very interesting" and that he would provide details after he finished in the clinic. He returned to the laboratory late in the day and began telling me about what he had learned at the meeting. The Navy was planning the world's largest antenna and was performing studies to help evaluate any possible health or environmental risks that the antenna's electromagnetic energy might pose. Paul Tyler formed the committee to evaluate about two dozen studies, most of which were not public knowledge, and convened the meeting to obtain a consensus interpretation of the initial results. Tyler and other Navy officials provided detailed information to the committee about the studies, and Dr. Becker said he would tell me about the good ones and about what the committee members said about them. He had taken notes and he glanced at them from time to time as he told me what happened.

In an experiment by Adey at UCLA, electromagnetic energy altered brain electrical activity in monkeys, "just like I found in salamanders ten years ago," Dr. Becker said. At the University of Minnesota, Halberg found that the energy altered biorhythms in insects, plants, and mice, indicating to Dr. Becker that living organisms could detect and respond to ultraweak energy levels which, with eyes wide, he remarked was exactly what Frank Brown had said many years earlier. I asked what the other committee members had to say about Adey's and Halberg's work. He didn't respond directly but rather began describing "the most amazing report of this kind of a response," by McCleave who worked at the University of Maine. Employing energy levels far lower than those that would be produced by the antenna, he showed that fish could detect the presence of the energy, a fact

McCleave had ascertained by continuously measuring the heart rate of the fish and showing that it changed immediately whenever he applied the energy. Dr. Becker called the experiment "clean" which I understood to mean that no one on the committee could suggest any cause for the change in heart rate other than the applied energy. Nevertheless a committee member named Justesen criticized the study, saying that it didn't pass the "laugh test" because the energy level was so low. Dr. Becker told me he told Justesen that the levels McCleave used were higher than the energy levels that the body used to regulate its activities, and asked Justesen, "Why would you think that McCleave's effects would be improbable?" Dr. Becker didn't remember Justesen's exact response; only that it was typical for an "establishment biologist."

A researcher from Illinois who investigated the impact of the antenna's energy on the migratory behavior of gulls reported that when he exposed the birds to the energy they became disoriented, a result that Dr. Becker took as support of his explanation for Twitty's observations on salamanders.

A study that interested Dr. Becker very much had been done by Noval, at a Navy laboratory in Pennsylvania. He found decreased growth rates in rats that had been exposed continuously to antenna-type energy. Not only that, changes occurred in four different biochemicals in the blood, indicating that the rats had experienced stress. Dr. Becker said that he told the committee that ongoing studies in his laboratory involving mice had led to similar results, and that he mentioned the results regarding stress that he and Howard Friedman had obtained several years earlier. It turned out that Polk, from Rhode Island, didn't find any effects on the growth of chickens due to the same energy levels Noval used. Several committee members argued that the two studies were contradictory because it wasn't possible that the energy could affect mice but not chickens. When Dr. Becker told me that detail he took a deep breath, I suppose to help cope with the stupidity of the argument, and I saw a vein on the right side of his forehead that I hadn't noticed a few moments earlier.

Tyler told the committee that a test version of the antenna that spanned several miles in Wisconsin had been operating for more than three years. Routine blood tests of sailors who worked at the test facility had uncovered elevated levels of some biochemicals related to stress and digestion. Those results prompted the Navy to conduct a human experiment at Pensacola in which sailors were exposed continuously for several days to simulated antenna energy. The physicians in charge of the experiment found differences in the same biochemicals in the blood of the exposed sailors compared with that of sailors who weren't exposed to the energy.

A wide range of biological effects caused by very low levels of electromagnetic energy had been uncovered, findings that Dr. Becker interpreted as empirical confirmation of his growth-control theory. He viewed the body as an intimately interconnected network rather than a series of independent parts like beads on a string, so he had predicted the kind of results disclosed at the meeting. But his viewpoint always generated intense opposition from classically trained biologists, so I asked him about how the other committee members reacted to the information the Navy officials had provided.

"The general attitude was that it was far-fetched to suggest such low energy levels could cause effects."

"They actually said that?"

"They used the typical code words, the usual crap," he said, and then began reading some of the comments he had recorded. 'Not all the animals reacted the same,' 'not all the tests were statistically significant,' 'the thresholds for the effects weren't established,' 'there were no mechanisms that could explain the results,' 'there may have been deficiencies in experimental design,' 'the results were somewhat inclusive,' 'more studies with larger number of animals are needed.' After reading all this he looked up from his notes and made one of the little speeches he sometimes made when he seemed to be trying to inculcate in me an appreciation for the complexity of living systems.

"Most people who do an experiment in biology expect to get a particular result. If they don't get it they assume that their thinking was wrong. They don't dare let themselves think their reasoning was sound but that the problem was the assumptions they reasoned from. If they could bring themselves to look up, they might see that there is something wrong with the system of thinking they learned and then used to generate the particular expectation. But they don't think about changes in the system, like slaves chained in a galley. So the system doesn't change."

"What about the kind of people who don't start that way?" I asked.

"When they begin an experiment they have hopes that don't come from dogma."

"From where, then?"

"From anywhere. From dreams, guesses, instinct. But when they use the method of science and prove that what they hoped for actually occurred, that result is valid even if the establishment mavens didn't expect it, don't like it, or can't explain it. It's a way of thinking that puts a premium on whether something is true, not on why it is true. But when they do get the results they hoped for, they must confront the established experts who reject results precisely because they are unexpected. Those people believe that if your results don't fit their theory, your results must be wrong, and that it is not incumbent on them to explain what they see as your errors. In grant committees and reviews of papers they use vicious words. Their purpose is not to just deny a grant or reject a paper, it is to kill the investigator's initiative. I have always fought against that perspective, and always will."

"So it was a disappointing meeting," I said.

"The opposite," he said with such force that I moved back a little in my chair. I didn't say anything, and during the lull he re-lit his pipe before continuing: "The Navy spent a lot of money for the research. I don't suppose they expected the results they got, but they got them anyway. They aren't stupid, they know that in the face of those results they can't expose half the people in Wisconsin unless they sort through all the problems and uncertainties in the research."

Several months later, I had a conversation with him a day after I had returned from a meeting in San Francisco.

"I heard a presentation by Jaffe," I said.

"Who?"

"The unpleasant embryologist from Purdue who confronted you during dinner at the meeting in New York."

"What did he say?"

"He described his attempts to induce frogs to grow new limbs using electromagnetic energy. He got poor results, which he blamed on the lack of funding. He said NIH wouldn't support his work because 'amateurs who don't know anything about regeneration research are poisoning the well.' He named you and Steve Smith as the persons he had in mind."

"That's not the first time someone has gone off on a mindless rant concerning my work, and it won't be the last," Dr. Becker replied.

"Perhaps you could do something to reduce that kind of opposition. The less frequent or nasty it is, the better the chances your ideas will gain acceptance by the establishment, or at least get a fair hearing."

"Do something? What?" he asked.

"At the meeting there was a symposium about the ideas of someone named Velikovsky. Have you ever heard of him?"

"Yes," he replied. " He claimed that earth and Venus had once collided. His theory was based on written accounts in ancient religious texts, and he was strongly attacked by the astronomy establishment. I heard Carl Sagan do that at a meeting. He went after Velikovsky because he is a psychiatrist and didn't get his ideas by using the methods that astronomers use."

"After Velikovsky gave his talk," I said, "Sagan and other astronomy professors spoke against him. It was a lynching, but there were people in the audience who supported Velikovsky, or at least who didn't like the kangaroo court that occurred."

"Undoubtedly they weren't astronomers," he said.

"Suppose Velikovsky had contacted astronomers before the meeting and talked to them about his methods. He might have found someone who appreciated their novelty, or who at least was willing to give him a fair hearing, not just call him a lot of bad names. Then, over time, he might have been perceived less as a threat to what they believed, which would tend to help gain some acceptance of his ideas."

"Sagan and the head of astronomy at Harvard happily call themselves his enemy," Dr. Becker answered. "How do you expect an 80-year-old MD who has zero funding to fight against them?"

"He can't, I suppose, it's too late for him. But I think you can. Some researchers speak warmly to you at meetings. You have three NIH grants. You publish often in the world's premier journals. On the one hand all this is strong evidence that in some sense your work is accepted. On the other hand, you are constantly confronting new establishments where you are not accepted and have no friends because no one knows you personally. Perhaps now is the time to adapt to the social realities. If you were to concentrate on a particular area and reach out to experts in that area and seek their advice, they would likely respect you for your wisdom even if your methods and results might tend to put them off. Forming contacts with such people could help you advance your agenda."

"You are suggesting that I make friends and try to persuade them by appealing to their individual pet ideas," he replied pointedly.

"I suggest that as one path forward," I answered, already sensing that my attempt to help him would not end well.

"Persuasion is something for people who would do or say anything, like a politician, or would put up with anything. I have no interest in doing anything like that. I'm not running for office or seeking membership in a cult, I'm trying to find useful facts and generate knowledge that can help solve human problems. You have been here long enough to know that I would never play their game."

***

During the same week in May that I finished law school, Dr. Becker got a call from Marguerite Hays, who had recently been appointed head of the VA division that funded both his appointment as a Medical Investigator and the major part of the laboratory itself. She told him she had received a letter from Jaffe in which he raised "troubling issues" and she asked for an explanation of his relationship to Jaffe. Dr. Becker replied that they had none and demanded to see the letter. Hays refused, telling him "there is no need to take the matter any further," but a friend in Central Office sent him a copy and when he read it he got very angry, a reaction that I think you will understand after I tell you what Jaffe wrote.

Jaffe claimed that the rapidity of the limb regeneration in the rats Dr. Becker had described in his *Nature* article was "implausible in the extreme because even a salamander, the regenerator par excellence, doesn't grow a new limb that quickly." Jaffe declared the "inescapable conclusion" that Dr. Becker had fabricated his data because "there is an extensive literature that rules out the possibility that the reported effects could have occurred." Jaffe said he discussed his views with other embryologists at Purdue and they all agreed that Dr. Becker's work completely lacked credibility, and the fact that it was published in *Nature* indicated only that the journal's editorial review procedures were inadequate. Jaffe explained that he wrote the letter to the VA because he felt he had a responsibility to expose bad science whenever it occurs. Otherwise, he said, "hopes are raised by unsupportable claims, public patience grows thin, and research support grows thin." A notation at the bottom of the letter indicated that Jaffe had sent copies to officials at NIH.

After telling me about the call and showing me the letter, Dr. Becker asked if I thought it was libelous. I downplayed the notion of legal action, listing various practical and technical reasons for my opinion, and then we began talking about what could or should be done to protect his reputation in the eyes of the NIH officials who received the letter.

"It seems clear," I said, "that professors in the regeneration establishment care only about salamanders and frogs and think your idea that a mammal can grow a new limb is nonsense. Jaffe is just one example."

He agreed.

"So your appeal needs to be to researchers who care about people."

"That is what I have always tried to do. I published two papers on rats, mammals, far closer to human beings than are frogs."

"That's not enough. They won't change their attitude toward you unless you present evidence that is convincing beyond a reasonable doubt."

"What are you saying, that I should do the experiment again?"

"Not only once more, many times more."

"No journal would publish the same result over and over."

"You have often said that journal editors favor baby steps and loathe novelty. You called it 'publishing the same thing over and over,' but it's really not because people who do it make small changes each time they repeat the work. You could use rabbits instead of rats, both genders not just males, increase or decrease the level of the applied energy, apply it for longer or shorter periods, or use different methods to measure the responses. The possibilities are almost limitless. Taking baby steps would obscure the novelty of your work because your critics would see only a small change between successive studies."

"That would be a fraud on the public which pays for what we do," he said. "I can hardly think of doing anything worse."

"But it would be good for you. Your work wouldn't strike fear and hatred in the hearts of conventional biologists. You would seem less alien and they would be more kindly disposed toward you when they sit on the NIH committees that review your applications for funding. And the NIH politicians who run the review committees would be less fearful of controversy because, as you have often said, they fund applications from researchers whose objectives are to fill in the small details."

"Your idea is preposterous," he said. "The work would be boring, and I couldn't finish it in my lifetime. If two publications don't motivate others to repeat my experiments, do you think that more than two would do that? I think not."

In December 1974 Dr. Becker received a brief but shocking letter from NIH informing him that the NIH grant he had had for twelve years had been terminated. No reasons were given. When he sought an explanation he was told only that his work lacked clarity and direction, that his experimental procedures hadn't been spelled out in enough detail, and that his results had generated "untoward controversy."

He began a series of clinical studies in which he applied very low levels of electromagnetic energy to patients, far lower than any other physician anywhere in the world who was doing similar clinical research. His objective was to cure infected non-unions, a disease notorious for being labor-intensive to manage and resistant to cure by means of conventional therapy. The source of the electromagnetic energy was what his patients called the "Becker Box." Using the Box, he achieved considerable clinical success, but the effort consumed much of his stamina and occupied much of his time. We all saw pretty clearly that the therapy he was developing was incapable of leading to a major clinical impact because managing the Box required too much physician time. And he was disclosing his methods as he developed them, so there was no possibility that his work could be patented for commercial development. Nevertheless he persisted in his studies of the effectiveness of the Box.

***

One day Dr. Becker told me a lawyer named Robert Simpson was coming to the laboratory. During a meeting, Simpson explained that a copy of a letter Dr. Becker had sent to state officials concerning possible public-health problems caused by powerlines had been forwarded to him because his agency regulated power companies, and he asked Dr. Becker to elaborate on what he had written. He told Simpson that the Navy intended to construct a large antenna that would produce electromagnetic signals detectable by submerged submarines, and in response to federal environmental laws, it had funded about twenty-four different biological studies to search for possible biological effects of the energy in the signals, even though none was expected because the energy levels were very low. A committee was appointed to evaluate the results of the studies, and he was selected as a member because he had performed research in the area, and had been an advisor to other government departments that were also interested in the effects of electromagnetic energy. When the committee met and learned about the results of the first year of experimentation, they had some misgivings about the safety of the antenna, which the Navy had named Sanguine, but expressed more serious concerns about a different issue. During a discussion of the actual levels of electromagnetic energy that would be produced by the Sanguine antenna, the committee learned that they were only a tiny fraction of those produced by high-voltage powerlines. Dr. Becker told Simpson the committee recommended that the Navy notify the proper state officials about the implications of the Sanguine results for the safety of high-voltage powerlines. "That recommendation prompted my letter," he said. Simpson replied that as far as he knew no state agency had received information from the Navy concerning the studies. He then explained that two New York companies were seeking licenses to build powerlines that would operate at three quarters of a million volts, and that legal proceedings regarding the license were in progress.

We began talking about how the energy levels of the antenna compared with those of powerlines. Reading from various reports and copies of testimony by power-company engineers, Simpson listed the levels expected at various distances from the centerline of the right-of-way because, of course, the levels would be lower the farther one moved away from the centerline. We soon realized that the powerline level didn't decrease to the Sanguine level until one was more than a thousand feet away. There was another dimension to the discussion that hadn't been mentioned so I said, "The energy levels of a powerline are present permanently because powerlines are designed to transport energy. But an antenna doesn't send out energy all the time because it is designed for communications. So if you are worried about the amount of exposure, you need to take into account that the dose of electromagnetic energy is probably determined by multiplying the energy level by the duration of exposure. For example, exposure to one gauss for one second may be biologically equivalent to exposure to a thousandth of a gauss for a thousand seconds." Dr. Becker bumped his fist on the table as if to add an exclamation point but said nothing.

Simpson said company engineers had testified that the powerlines would be completely safe regardless of the duration of exposure or how close one was to the powerline, assuming of course that a person didn't actually touch the wires. That information surprised and irritated Dr. Becker, and he told Simpson that his and other published studies in biomedical science, together with the results of the Navy studies, had led him to suspect the possibility of side-effects. He couldn't say for certain there would be side-effects, but he was certain that the engineers were "plain wrong" when they said that the present state of the science proved that the powerlines would be safe. Not nearly enough research had been done, he said, to justify that claim. He advised Simpson to contact the Navy to obtain the latest information so that he could see for himself there were many reasons why what the engineers said was untrue. Then in a clear and pointed tone he said, "If Sanguine-level energy can cause biological effects, what the hell do you expect will happen at much higher levels for much longer exposure times? Nothing good I think."

Simpson explained that his job in the proceedings was to represent the people of the state. If it appeared to him that there was a viable alternative position to that advanced by the companies, his responsibility was to present that position to the judge. He said he believed that Dr. Becker's opinion concerning the medical consequences of exposure to the powerline energy ought to be presented, and he asked Dr. Becker if he would serve the state as an expert witness.

After Simpson left to return to Albany I asked Dr. Becker whether he really intended to testify.

"Yes," he said, "assuming that they also extend an invitation to you to testify."

"Why do you want to testify?" I asked. "It's risky, and there is already a lot on your plate."

"It would be a good opportunity to show the public the importance of research," he answered, took several puffs on his pipe, and then said, "If people understood that the kind of research we are doing could help identify what makes them sick, then it would be more likely that our research would be supported. The NIH took away my grant. We lost three good people. Unless new funding appears from somewhere, the lab will slowly die."

"You mean that your testimony would raise public awareness of health risks from electromagnetic energy?"

"I hope it would do far more than that."

"What do you mean?"

"The system doesn't ask the right questions."

"You think that testifying will change that?"

"It might," he replied, "but whatever happens I think it is something I must do."

"The companies will hire top lawyers who will not treat you well when you testify, and there will be nobody to help you."

"Simpson will be there," he replied.

"But his employer is a state agency and his client is the public, not you. There is a difference."

"I'm not concerned. I will know more about the subject than the lawyers."

His request for permission to testify was approved by Central Office and by Max Cleland, the director of the VA, with the proviso that Dr. Becker clearly indicate his opinions were his own and not those of the VA. Several long-time workers at the hospital who were friends of Dr. Becker told him stories about what had happened to people at other VA hospitals who had tried to do what they believed was the right thing. The workers told Dr. Becker that the politicians in Central Office would turn against him at the first sign of trouble. But he gave no indication that what they said had any effect on his plans. "My mind is made up," he told them.

With Simpson's guidance Dr. Becker prepared a written report in a question-and-answer format that described his opinions about the potential health impacts of the electromagnetic energy that would be produced by the proposed powerlines. In response to a question about the purpose of his research, he said that he was trying to elucidate the details of the control systems that living organisms utilize to direct certain basic life functions such as growth, healing, and biological cycles. Then he answered other questions:

Q. What have you been experimenting on, and for how long?

A. For the past 15 years we have been studying the effects on animals caused by a variety of different kinds of electromagnetic energy.

Q. What is your overall conclusion?

A. The results of our experiments conclusively indicated that electromagnetic energy has an effect upon living organisms. As we predicted based on the physical nature of the biological electronic control system, external electromagnetic energy, both natural and man-made, can produce physiological and functional changes in living organisms.

Q. How do these results come about?

A. The basic reason is that the body has an electrical system which controls growth and healing, and is probably related to the perception of pain. There is evidence that the system also links biological cycles of behavior exhibited by humans and animals to the cyclic patterns of environmental electromagnetic energy that occur in nature. The solid-state properties of the cells of this electrical control system are such that it would be influenced by changes in the level of electromagnetic energy in the environment.

Q. Would such reactions occur in response to man-made as well as natural electromagnetic energy?

A. Yes.

Q. Could changes occur in response to the electromagnetic energy from the proposed powerlines?

A. The strength of those energy levels and the duration of the exposure that they will produce are both far beyond the levels and durations which result from any other source of electromagnetic energy that man has ever built. Consequently the proposed powerlines pose the highest risk of such changes.

Q. Please explain how you think those changes could come about.

A. Exposure to electromagnetic energy differing in frequency and/or in magnitude from the normal earth's field may produce biological effects by inducing small levels of electrical energy within the tissues that could interfere with normal healing and growth processes by presenting abnormal signals to the tissues. Another possible process is by interfering with the normal biological cyclic rhythm through interaction with the electrical system linking organisms to the geophysical environment.

Q. What is the medical significance of your conclusion?

A. From a medical viewpoint, our work and that of many others described in the literature represents a solid body of data indicating that living organisms are influenced by electromagnetic energy, and that such effects are likely to occur in the areas of growth, both cellular and of the total organism, and in the function of the central nervous system and cardiovascular system. The effects could occur directly, as when the energy interacts with a particular tissue and causes it to change from healthy to diseased tissue, or they could occur indirectly, as for example a stress response. Obviously, to answer particular questions such as the specific effects of different durations of exposure to various strengths of electromagnetic energy upon the health of the variable human population will require specific laboratory experimentation. These answers are not available at this time.

Q. What is a stress response?

A. It is a particular kind of systemic response to an environmental stimulus. Stress denotes a condition in which the body deviates from its normal resting state because of the occurrence of the environmental factor, which is called a stressor. In this model of disease causation, the stressor causes the stress and the stress wears down the body's resistance to disease. This theory is generally accepted as a useful framework to explain some diseases and to design experiments.

Q. Is electromagnetic energy from powerlines a stressor?

A. Many of the scientific reports, particularly those from Project Sanguine, are interpretable in this light. Environmental electromagnetic energy is directly linked to the living organisms via the electronic control system we have described. Changes in the energy level, especially increased strength and frequencies not normally present, can produce stress in exposed organisms.

Q. Is that harmful?

A. Since the effects we noted experimentally indicated that the applied energy acted as a stressor, I would have to assume that the effects would be harmful.

While working with Simpson in preparing the report, Dr. Becker explained his view that indiscriminate exposure of an unknowing public to electromagnetic energy was unethical. He said that if he wanted to apply electromagnetic energy to human subjects in an experiment, he would be ethically and legally required to follow stringent rules designed to protect the research subjects. The foremost of these rules was the requirement that the subject give written informed consent. The power companies, however, were seeking permission from the state to be allowed to apply electromagnetic energy without following the informed-consent rule or any of the other rules. He emphasized that what the companies planned to do was involuntary human research, because they would be testing their theory that unlimited exposure would be completely safe. Moreover they would be doing so without telling the subjects about the experiment or the risk. He called the situation "Kafkaesque."

Simpson was taken aback by Dr. Becker's argument because he felt he might be presenting testimony that seemed to argue that the power companies were like Nazis. Simpson and Dr. Becker had a long discussion in which they went back and forth regarding how the fundamental inconsistency Dr. Becker saw could be presented in a non-inflammatory fashion. Ultimately they settled on a format in which Simpson would ask Dr. Becker to explain what human research was and what rules were followed. He would answer by saying that human research was the use of human beings as test subjects to answer an existing scientific question, and that federal regulations required a committee of experts to review any proposed study in detail. It was the responsibility of the committee to balance risks against gains of any given experiment before approving the proposed study. The most important rules were that the experiment be clearly and fairly explained to subjects, particularly with regard to all the risks, and that the experiment should not be done until the subject has given full and informed consent.

In Dr. Becker's final report Simpson asked questions that elicited these opinions. And then he asked:

Q. Would it be considered medically unethical to apply electromagnetic energy like that from the proposed powerlines to humans for research purposes without securing their permission?

A. Yes, it would be considered unethical in my opinion, because exposure is not without risks to health.

Q. Would it be considered medically unethical to apply electromagnetic energy to humans for any purpose or even no purpose without securing their permission?

A. Yes, it would be considered unethical in my opinion, if the field strengths exceeded that to which we are exposed in the normal course of everyday living. In that case approval of the human experimentation committee and informed consent would be required.

Q. Do you believe that the proposed powerlines would be safe if they were built as presently designed?

A. No, for the reason that its electromagnetic energy level will be in the range possibly productive of biological effects. I believe that chronic exposure of humans to such levels should be viewed as human experimentation, and subjected to the rules previously mentioned. I believe that the most prudent course to follow would be to determine the complete spectrum of biological effects produced by exposure to powerline energy. It should then be possible to establish firm levels of permitted exposure with regard to both the energy levels and the permissible duration of exposure.

Dr. Becker's report was unique in American jurisprudence, a rationally based and ethically motivated assessment of the impact of commercial activities on human health, submitted in a legal proceedings where the assessment could be tested by cross-examination under oath by adversaries who had virtually limitless legal and technical resources. Within about a month of when Simpson sent the report to the power companies, they formally requested that the legal proceedings be delayed for a year so that they could prepare what they told him was "a complete and thorough response that will show Dr. Becker's testimony is factually and legally incorrect and erroneous." Simpson's agency granted the request and also greatly expanded the scope of the proceedings by inviting all the power companies in the state to participate and to respond to the issues Dr. Becker had raised.

Local newspapers along the route of the planned powerlines published excerpts from the report. His views were advanced in other proceedings where powerlines were being built, and in disputes that developed regarding the risks of existing powerlines, a potential area of controversy so large it could put the ongoing proceedings in the shade. Opponents of the Sanguine antenna used his report as further evidence against the Navy project. Melvin Laird, the US secretary of defense, moved the antenna from Wisconsin, his state, to the Upper Peninsula in Michigan, a development that Dr. Becker somehow knew about before it was announced publicly.

Dr. Becker seemed satisfied with the overall legal and public response, which he saw as the beginning of a national awakening from the dogmatic slumber that equated almost breathless ignorance of the consequences of chronic exposure to man-made electromagnetic energy on human health with conclusive proof of complete safety. But none of the Sanguine researchers or any of the researchers whose publications he had cited in his report spoke publicly about the implications of their work. "That would have been nice," he said, "but I'm not surprised."

Bassett and Brighton, who were developing commercial medical applications for electromagnetic energy, remained publicly silent regarding Dr. Becker's report, even though journalists repeatedly asked them for their opinions. Both surgeons said only that man-made medically purposed electromagnetic energy was good or at worst did nothing, but under no circumstances had any bad effects. You might wonder why physicians generally didn't speak out concerning the health risks, but if you reflect on the relation between medicine and experimental biology you will realize that clinicians never lead but always follow the lead of experimental biologists. Clinicians do not accept knowledge claims until they have been blessed by experimental biologists. But they had never embraced Dr. Becker's non-reductionist methods nor the results he obtained when he employed them, and unsurprisingly the academicians did not embrace the societal implications he extracted from those results and they said so when interviewed by reporters. I told Dr. Becker I thought that at least some in the scientific community would have supported him. "What community?" he replied.

Lionel Jaffe

Chapter 10.
Crises

1975–1976: He studies the health risks of electromagnetic energy, is cross-examined in court, and loses his appointment as a Medical Investigator

Dr. Becker continued his animal experiments aimed at proving that powerline electromagnetic energy could cause physiological changes, believing that the results of the experiments would help spur the government to "determine the complete spectrum of biological effects produced by exposure to powerline energy." Such knowledge, he thought, would lead to an appropriate regulatory scheme and ultimately to decreased levels of disease. Cast in terms of the null-hypothesis model of experimental biology, his hypothesis was that exposure to electromagnetic energy caused biological effects in animals, and his null hypothesis was that it didn't. But at the prestigious institutions of biology in the United States, testing hypotheses of this type was called "phenomenology" and regarded as barely scientific, suitable only for commercial research like that involving the side-effects of drugs or the hazards of toxic chemicals used in food or cosmetics. Nobody prior to Dr. Becker had ever proposed phenomenology as a first-line strategy to study the side-effects of man-made electromagnetic energy. Looking back now and trying to understand his motivation at this stage of his career, I remember a story he told me. One day his father gave young Robert a paper bag containing DDT and told him to fumigate their garage. Repeatedly shaking the bag inside the garage produced a white cloud of DDT, some of which he unavoidably inhaled while never suspecting that it could harm him. Years later, after learning about the dangers of DDT, he wondered what the long-term consequences to his health might have been. The experience may have helped give rise to his life-long interest in preventive medicine.

Establishment biologists had little tolerance for experiments that were rationalized based on considerations of preventive medicine. "They don't do disease prevention, they do mechanisms," was the way he once made that point. Their approach to the issue of the interaction of electromagnetic energy with tissue, if they ever considered the subject at all, would have required the investigator to critically analyze past studies and on that basis to hypothesize a particular biochemical that would be altered by exposure to the energy. Then the investigator would be expected to show to a statistical certainty that the average amount of the biochemical differed between animals that were or were not exposed. In the published narrative the investigator would be required to eliminate all other possible explanations for the putative causal relationship, and also to describe a mechanism by which the energy caused the effect. Dr. Becker thought this approach produced only publishable knowledge, not solutions to existential human problems such as what caused disease, and what constituted a cure. In his eyes the establishment approach was methodologically incomplete and not the most important thing a scientist could do.

You can understand, at least partly, why the approaches of Dr. Becker and the establishment biologists differed if you ponder their deepest motivations. He believed that his highest moral responsibility was to prevent and cure disease, which could be done efficaciously only by identifying the underlying causal factors. He therefore sought answers to a finite number of causal questions using integrative experimental designs. In contrast, the academicians believed in *scientia est scientia*, the pursuit of which was the route to professional advancement. They sought answers to an infinite number of mechanistic questions using reductionist experimental designs, but had no expectation that the knowledge in their publications would be useful and no criteria for ranking its relative importance. He recognized that their work had some value but believed it was of lesser importance. They believed there was no value in what he did. So you can see there existed fundamental differences regarding values.

In some animal experiments we measured endpoints that could reasonably be expected to reflect cumulative consequences of constant exposure to electromagnetic energy. He reasoned on the basis of common sense that changes in those endpoints would indicate hazards irrespective of what specific biochemical mechanisms were involved. Thinking this way he decided that body weight and death rate in mice were good endpoints because they were universally accepted as important measures of health. In rat experiments, based on his theory that the constant presence of electromagnetic energy was a stressor, we measured alterations in the biochemicals and organs that were known to be part of the stress-response system. In both kinds of experiments we repeatedly found the effects he predicted. Simpson sent the information to the power companies and told them it would be described in Dr. Becker's testimony, and in mine.

In the spring of 1976 Richard Phillips, a biochemist and employee of a research-for-hire company in Washington state, visited our laboratory. He told us about contracts that his company had with a consortium consisting of the Electric Power Research Institute, the US Department of Energy, and various US power companies, the purposes of which were to repeat our research that Simpson had disclosed, and to measure a huge range of other biological endpoints. The contracts were intended to support more than twenty people for at least three years, with overall budgets that were a thousand times higher than the entire budget for our laboratory. Phillips unabashedly told us what he expected would be his ultimate conclusion. "We did more experiments, more carefully, using better equipment, measuring more endpoints and found no effects." Dr. Becker did not believe that would happen. Furthermore for fifteen years he had pleaded for other researchers to repeat his experiments if they did not accept his results. So he was glad to learn that was exactly what Phillips planned to do. But Phillips was not an academician doing *scientia est scientia* while enjoying the privilege of academic freedom, but rather an employee of a company seeking to make a profit and satisfy the needs of the other parties to the contracts, like a builder who constructs a house according to the design of his client. After Phillips departed I expressed my concern regarding his compromised position, but Dr. Becker dismissed it. My concern and his dismissal turned out to be irrelevant because the depravity of Phillips' research was so great there was absolutely nothing we could have done in response.

On the Saturday night a week before he was to testify, Dr. Becker and his wife Lillian hosted a party at their house for the laboratory staff, an annual event in the spring after all the snow had melted and the road on the hill where he lived was passable without needing a pick-up truck with a snow plow. When I had the opportunity to speak with her out of his earshot I asked whether she thought he was ready to take the witness stand and undergo cross-examination by the power companies. She told me he was "very much looking forward to talking with the lawyers," and that she thought it would be a "rewarding experience," smiling as she spoke. She knew I had already testified for many days and asked if I felt that way. I demurred rather than raise concerns by answering truthfully, and offered to provide him tactical advice if that were his wish.

During the next week Dr. Becker and I spoke about the results of the experiments on rats, particularly the stress hormones that we measured using a spectrophotofluorometer he purchased for that purpose, but we never spoke about how best to deal with the hostility he was certain to encounter or the frustration he would feel as the company lawyers cross-examined him, trying to find his Achilles heel.

Monday Testimony

The hearing room was lined with tables on the left and the right, a dozen lawyers and gofers representing the power companies sitting on the left and Simpson sitting alone on the right. The judge, Thomas Matias, sat at a desk on an elevated platform from which he peered down at the lawyers and at the witness stand to his left, off the platform. Because Dr. Becker would not agree to go to Albany to testify, Matias and the lawyers had to schlep 150 miles down the Thruway to Syracuse, a situation that palpably aggravated them. When the hearing began the lawyers entered their objections on the record, arguing that many people had been inconvenienced solely for the benefit of Dr. Becker. Matias apologized to the lawyers but said that his superiors had ordered him to hear Dr. Becker in Syracuse.

Dr. Becker took the witness stand with an air of confidence, and the pattern for the cross-examination was quickly established. A lawyer would ask a series of questions whereupon he would sit down and another lawyer would pop up and continue the questioning, sometimes in a disrespectful tone, like a game of whack-a-mole. Although Dr. Becker's sarcasm flared occasionally in response to provocations, mostly he was courteous and courtly.

Q. Why isn't the material in your report in the textbooks of biology?

A. The branch of physics known as solid-state physics really began to be developed following World War II. This led to the devices such as a transistor where you are able to do things with much smaller voltages and much smaller currents. Now, the application of this concept in biology as opposed to electronics began at a lecture given by Dr. Szent-Gyorgyi in which he pointed out the concept that very small currents and voltages could control biological functions, and that this would require rethinking of solid-state structures in biological terms. Up until that time, the cell was viewed sort of as a cellophane bag full of vegetable soup, and everything took place in an aqueous environment. Many investigators looked into the area of biological solid state, and this constitutes a body of literature which is developing. So no one really knows enough to write a book on it yet, but it is in the journals.

Q. Doctor, you said, "We have determined that living organisms possess certain electric control systems characterized by the use of very small electric currents and voltages and control signals." Hasn't that concept been known for 100 years?

A. No, sir, I hope not because that is the concept that we feel we have developed.

Q. Doctor, you asserted that limited funds are the reason for a lack of confirmatory reports of research results of other investigators whose work you cited. Is your claim based upon any documentation?

A. That is a good question and there is a good answer. I was referring to the fact that there is one study that describes the occurrence of bone tumors in exposed animals, and I stated that the investigator operated on a limited budget and within a specific frame of reference. And he was not primarily interested in the occurrence of bone tumors. That was not why he performed the experiment. The tumors appeared as unexpected side-effects. These possibilities may explain why he did not repeat the study.

Q. Now, Doctor, are you referring in that particular response only to the particular investigator, or are you referring to other investigators in the scientific community who might also confirm or deny the validity of the results obtained?

A. I am referring generically to investigators and to research programs. Every program that there is has a certain limit on funds which restricts what you can do, primarily because of the limitation on personnel and equipment and so forth. Every program also has stated objectives and aims, and the results will always be examined for their relevance to those stated objectives and aims.

Q. Doctor, in your opinion, is it equally possible that the lack of con-firmatory reports results from either a scientist's disbelief of the results in the report or their inability to confirm the results, though attempts were made inasmuch as negative reports are not often published?

A. I think I can give you an answer in regards to the bone-tumor ex-periment which, to the best of my knowledge, has not been repeated. One of the reasons why this has not occurred is because it is extremely difficult to get funding for research that does not fit into the establishment's frame of reference. I worked fairly closely with Dr. Bassett at Columbia and he informed me that he had forwarded to, I believe it was the National In-stitutes of Health, a project proposal designed to evaluate in a controlled laboratory circumstance not only the possibility of the production of tu-mors by certain kinds of electromagnetic energy, but also the effect that the energy would have on pre-existing tumors. The project proposal was rejected out-of-hand by the National Institutes of Health as having no foundation. That decision reflected the then extant opinion that tumors were caused by either viruses or immunological deficiencies of some sort and therefore, within the operating framework of the National Institutes of Health, it would have been impossible, or practically impossible to get funding for a project such as this. So you have a gamut of possibilities as to why any specific experiment has not been either refuted or substantiated in the literature.

Q. Doctor, you referred to the difficulty in getting funding which does not fall into the establishment's idea of general lines of research. Would you characterize your own research as falling outside the lines of the establish-ment's generally accepted research approach?

A. When I began the studies quite a few years ago, they certainly did fall outside the establishment's viewpoint. At the present time, however, in my own opinion, we have demonstrated a number of validities to our ap-proach that are clinically relevant and important, and I don't believe that at the present time our total research scope could be considered to be outside the establishment's lines of considered validity.

Q. You said that the complete spectrum of biological effects produced by exposure to powerline energy should be determined. Could you give us your estimate of how many years of research that would require?

A. It is always very dangerous to predict how long any research is going to take because research basically means that you do not know what your results are going to be. In my own opinion, for what that might be worth, I think the questions relative to the hazards of any given level of energy could be answered within something between two to six years of study.

Q. In your estimate, how long would it take for laboratory experimentation which you suggested to establish the answers for all levels of energy?
A. I would expect that might take longer than the two to six years.

Q. Now, in your report, you discuss the ethics involved in exposing humans without their consent, and you discuss the whole problem of human experimentation, do you not?
A. Yes.

Q. You mention that before a case of human experimentation can be prosecuted, the present regulations require that any proposed study be reviewed in detail by a committee of experts including medical and scientific personnel.
A. Yes, the National Institute of Health has published a set of regulations governing human experimentation. I believe the World Health Organization has done likewise.

Q. What criteria are employed to determine whether a human experiment is in fact being conducted?
A. If you have an experiment and your subject is human, that is human experimentation.

Q. For example, when they tested the atomic bomb in the western desert flats, was that an example of human experimentation?
A. By present criteria it certainly would be.

Q. It would be today, but it was not then; is that right?
A. That's correct; yes, sir.

Q. When a new model comes out in a car, is that an example of a human experimentation?

MR. SIMPSON: Your Honor, I'm going to object. This is ridiculous. The witness isn't here to offer opinions about cars.

JUDGE: Sustained.

Q. What do you mean by "if it affects human beings, it's deemed a human experiment?" Can you give us a little better description of what you mean by that term?

A. An experiment, per se, is doing something to look for a result which you cannot with absolute certainty predict will occur. That's the nature of an experiment. If you're going to pursue your experiment with humans as the subjects, then that would be human experimentation. In the example you chose of the testing of the bomb, they were aware that there was a radiation danger. They could not accurately predict the results of the test, so under present regulations, this would be human experimentation. Even though it was in the military, some sort of informed consent on the part of the troops who were involved would be required.

Now, your other instance of a new model of an automobile — a

Q. You're vitiating your counsel's objection, you understand.

A. I know, but I think it's a good example. I don't think a new model of an automobile could be considered an experiment in the true sense of the word. We know what automobiles do. We know that there's a certain risk involved in their operation. I don't think any company deliberately sets out to manufacture a model the characteristics of which they really cannot reasonably accurately predict, so it's not an experiment in that case.

Q. It would be much like a new powerline, I gather?

A. No, I wouldn't say that.

After his testimony was finished for the day I said to him:

"When they ask you questions that go beyond what you agreed would be your area of testimony, don't try to answer, or make guesses. Tell them 'I don't know,' or 'I haven't thought about that,' or 'I don't have an opinion about that.'"

"What questions are you talking about?"

"For example, they asked you how long it would take to determine the complete spectrum of biological effects due to electromagnetic energy. The only way to answer that kind of question is to not answer it. But you told them two to six years, which now opens you up tomorrow to a new line of examination regarding the basis for your answer."

"The time estimate was appropriate and reasonable," he said. "I'm confident that it's correct."

"But you are only guessing. You have certain expertise, and when you testify in that area the court can regard your opinion as fact. But your expertise is not a license to guess. The lawyers will encourage you to engage in serial guessing, and at the end when they write their briefs they will argue that everything you said was a guess, including your testimony that the energy can cause biological effects. The more guesses you make, the more you strengthen their argument."

"I do not view this situation as an adversarial process," he said.

"You should, because that is exactly what it is," I replied.

"I don't think so. But whether or not the questions are honestly intended to obtain information, my responsibility is to provide the information because there are people who will read the transcripts who have no clue of the extent of the present problem."

"When the lawyers asked you whether you thought electric blankets were safe, their purpose wasn't to seek information but rather to help develop an argument that you are against modernity and want to return to the pre-electrical age. That's why they kept asking you about other electrical devices. That entire series of questions was unnecessary and could have been avoided if you told them 'I don't have any opinion about that.'"

"But I wanted to answer that question. Electric blankets don't involve exposure of the head, like powerlines. The stress response takes place because of changes that occur in the brain."

"The stress response may take place in the brain, but the detection process by which the body becomes aware that the electromagnetic energy is present may take place elsewhere. We don't know. If you continue answering as you did today, I mean suggesting that you do know, you may undercut your credibility."

"I don't see any problem because I think detection occurs in the brain," he replied.

Tuesday Testimony

He went to the hospital early in the morning to see his patients and then returned to the courtroom. His body language suggested less enthusiasm but more determination than the previous day.

Q. Yesterday you said that stress involves the brain and can lead to disease. Can you identify the source of your theory?

A. I think you have to understand that the concept of stress is one that has developed slowly over the years. Dr. Hans Selye in Montreal did a lot of work on stress and the physiological responses from stress. The majority of people who work in the field agree that a major portion of the response, whatever it may be, is the result of central nervous system action, so this is not solely my opinion.

Q. Doctor, it has been said that the biological response to stress can be "good for you." Is there some doubt that stress can cause a pathological state?

A. I don't believe there's any doubt that stress can cause a pathological state, nor do I think there's any doubt that certain amounts of stress are probably good for you. The question is the extent and the chronicity of the stress. Stresses are additive in a sense. Now, understand I use the term stress in a very wide sense. Let me take this opportunity to go a little further into this because I think you want to develop stress situations somewhat more.

Q. Surely.

A. There are certain physiological responses that are associated with a response to a stressful situation. These can now be identified in a wide variety of circumstances. The present concepts are that not only a few diseases but also the whole concept of disease in general is markedly influenced by mental mechanisms, by functions that take place within the brain. Now, the response to a situation is determined in part by what the animal or human perceives the situation to be and how they can react thereto. So it is quite conceivable that if you have circumstances that alter the functional state of the central nervous system, you could have then the same physiological responses that you see in a stressful situation. In other words, we may not be able to apply what the layman would say, "Well, this is stress and this is not stress." The organism may still respond in the same fashion and produce the same physiological responses solely because of some action at the level of the central nervous system.

Q. Do I correctly conclude that stress can take on a multiplicity of shapes and forms?

A. Exactly.

Q. And it's not your testimony that stresses emanate only from the electromagnetic energy that we are discussing; isn't that correct?

A. To carry that one step further, all that we can say is that the response of the animal to the energy is in keeping with a stressful response. This does not necessarily imply that the energy, per se, was stressful. The effect could have been a functional effect upon the central nervous system with subsequent alterations, the same as a stressful situation.

Q. Doctor, you have mentioned "multiple stresses." Could you define for us what you mean by that term?

A. Every time you have a pathological condition like an infection, the body mobilizes its resources to deal with the condition. This would be a single stress. Assume an individual has an infection of some sort, something that is not particularly life threatening but is productive of a response on the part of that organism that helps that organism to resist that disease. Then add to that another stress. Let's call it a social stress, loss of job, difficulty at home, this sort of thing. These are multiple stresses, and their effects are additive.

Q. In other words, a human being passing back and forth under a high-voltage powerline would not be an example of multiple stresses.

A. No. That would be an example of intermittent stress.

Q. Doctor, would electric blankets be biological stressors?

A. I cannot give you a direct answer for the following reasons: The definition of a biological stressor is a condition that will produce stress within the organism. The present concept of the production of stress response in an organism hinges upon events in the central nervous system itself. In other words, the brain is an essential organ for the generation of the stress response. As I indicated before, in general, the exposed individual has to perceive the stress. Now, all that we have found in our studies is that animals exposed to electromagnetic energy appear to have some of the physiological correlates of the stress syndrome. We cannot at all be certain at this time that this is produced by the animal perceiving the applied energy or whether or not the energy has a direct effect upon the central nervous system itself, producing as a second-order phenomenon the physiological alterations of stress. So I cannot precisely say that the energy from an electric blanket would be a stressor. The total body is not exposed. I imagine it varies from individual to individual. I haven't slept with my head under the covers in a long time—I will put it that way. If there is a single site wherein the energy has its specific effect, producing a physiological response akin to the stress response, this site may be in the brain. I cannot guess at what the energy level within the brain would be within an individual under an electric blanket. So I cannot say that that would in my lexicon definitely constitute an environmental stressor.

Q. In your report you said you were "Chief of Orthopedics" and a "Medical Investigator." How do those two jobs relate to one another?

A. One involves providing medical and surgical care for the patients, the other involves performing research. The Medical Investigator program in the VA is a special grant that supports physicians whose research is deemed particularly important for the veteran population.

Q. How is your time divided between the two jobs?

A. I am allowed to spend up to 75% of my time performing research, but I usually spend less time than that, depending on the number of patients and the workload of the orthopedists on my staff.

Q. What was your contribution to the multi-generation study of mice that Dr. Marino performed?

A. As part of the overall research project proposal that formed the basis for the Medical Investigator program, based upon previous work and analysis over fifteen years, I had synthesized a theory regarding the possible existence of additional control systems within living organisms that had specific types of functions. The theory would imply that electromagnetic energy in the vicinity of living organisms would have effects upon the function of these organisms. Based upon that theory which I presented on several occasions, I was invited by the Navy to be a member of an advisory committee. After the discussions in which I participated, I learned that there existed in the Navy studies evidence that corroborated the theory that I had held which apparently was the reason why I was invited to become a part of that committee. During a committee meeting the question of the possibility of effects upon humans as a result of the operations of the high-voltage powerlines was raised. Subsequently, I became aware of the fact that there were proposals to establish such powerlines in New York State. As a result of the two pieces of knowledge, I felt it incumbent upon me as a physician to express a measure of concern to state officials. This I did in the form of a letter, and we were subsequently contacted and requested to participate—

Q. Excuse me, Doctor. I think we are going far afield. I asked you what your input was to the study.

A. Before I give you the input, I have to give you some background.

MR. SIMPSON: I think the witness should be permitted to answer.
JUDGE: Go ahead, Dr. Becker.
THE WITNESS: Yes, sir. One of the tasks that I proposed in the research protocol in connection with the Medical Investigator program was to investigate the possible biological effects of electromagnetic energy. After being contacted and asked to testify, I realized that we could perhaps kill two birds with one stone. My original intent was to investigate the effects of zero frequency and very low frequency electromagnetic energy, which I predicted would cause major biological effects. These frequencies are within the region of 1 to 20 Hz. Then the question of the effect of Sanguine energy in the region between 45 and 75 Hz arose, which includes 60 Hz, the type of energy that comes from powerlines. Since the question whether there are any effects of 60-Hz energy produced by powerlines had arisen, and because Dr. Marino indicated to me that we could save considerable money if, instead of investigating the effects of between 1 and 20 Hz, we investigated the effects of 60 Hz, I instructed Dr. Marino to go ahead and to design and plan and execute appropriate experiments in this regard. As a result of that commission on my part to him, the studies came about.

Q. Could you tell us briefly what your participation was in the conduct of the mouse and rat experiments that Dr. Marino described?

A. My contribution is a very generalized one. For example, if you wished to evaluate the effect of an altered electromagnetic environment on a living organism, what sort of things should you look for? You can do an experiment and measure a thousand different things, and none of them might be changed due to the exposure. You have to make a prediction as to what sort of effects one would see, and my primary contribution to the work that Dr. Marino did was to steer him in the direction of looking for the physiological changes that would accompany stress. Now, that prediction was made based upon a wide variety of data in the literature, particularly the literature referring to biological cycles where there are at the present time two competing theories on the causative factors for biological cycles. One of those is that those cycles are triggered and the period set by the natural changes in the earth's natural electromagnetic environment so that if you altered the natural electromagnetic environment significantly for an animal, you would expect to see some evidence of an alteration in the animal's biological cycle pattern. Now, from other information that has been generated, we know that changes in biological cycling patterns are productive of what science presently terms the stress response syndrome, so my contribution was that if you're going to expose these animals, you have to look for signs of stress.

Q. If powerlines can cause health problems, wouldn't they have been manifested in persons exposed to existing powerlines?

A. What you're getting at is, I think, that there are energy levels at various points around existing powerlines that are stronger than those from these new powerlines. Am I paraphrasing you correctly?

Q. That's correct.

A. And what you're saying now is since these energy levels did exist, should we not have seen some effect?

Q. Precisely.

A. Well, the answer to that is that all of these effects are common effects in our population. It's not at all uncommon to have patients with hypertension, arteriosclerotic heart disease, and gastric duodenal ulcers. These are very common in our society at the present time. To say that they are or are not due to the existing levels of electromagnetic energy that these people are exposed to would require an epidemiological type of study. In that type of study you would have to take matched population groups within those fields of exposure and without these fields of exposure. There are a number of factors to be considered in the situation. The diseases that we see in medical practice today constitute a different class of disease than were the commonest diseases 40 or 50 years ago. Hypertension is a very common disease and I would suspect that increased irritability on the part of the general population is a very common condition, as evidenced by the consumption of tranquilizers in the United States at the present time. We have had the occurrence of medical conditions that you didn't see in the literature 50 years ago. Hyperactivity on the part of children, for example. A very discernible percentile of children in school in the United States are under treatment for what is called a hyperactivity syndrome. Now, all this came out of the air, all of a sudden. In the area of growth disturbance, there's an increase in the attack rate of malignancies in our population. So to say that these fields have existed since 1940 or 1950 and that apparently nothing has happened, I don't think that is correct. It is true that no one has their hair turned green and their eyeballs fall out when they stand underneath the transmission line, but whether or not the disease complex that we see in medicine today is or is not related thereto, I am not about to say at this time.

Q. Is what you're saying that these manifestations exist in the environment or among the population today, but that you can't relate these discernible effects to the fields generated by powerlines? Is that what you're telling us?

A. What I'm telling you is that the evidence that we have accumulated indicates that animals under control circumstances, if exposed to these parameters, will develop the physiological changes that we enumerated. That if you transfer this to the human population, then the same sort of thing would occur. I see no difference between rats and people in this regard. The question that then comes up is: if this is so, why haven't we seen it? I think this is what you are alluding to, and in that case all I can say is that no one has done the appropriate epidemiological study to establish this as the primary causative factor. This doesn't negate the possibility or the probability that this would occur.

Q. Isn't it true that you previously defined human experimentation as doing something to look for a result which you cannot, with absolute certainty, predict will occur and that if you pursue your experiment with humans as the subjects, that would be human experimentation, is that correct?

A. I think your quote was accurate.

Q. Would you consider the construction of a powerline as doing something to look for a result?

A. If I understand your question correctly, I don't think you could characterize it as that.

Q. Well, then, the building of a powerline would not be human experimentation, would it, inasmuch as it is not being built in order to look for a result that you cannot with absolute certainty predict?

A. Well, I think the construction of the powerline certainly is not an experiment. That is obvious in itself. The operation of the powerline and the exposure of individuals to energy levels in excess of those we have used before, in my opinion, would constitute an experiment.

At the end of the day, after Dr. Becker had left the witness stand, Simpson told Matias that Dr. Becker had honored his commitment to testify, and that he now needed to be excused from the case so that he could return to his duties at the hospital. The power-company lawyers complained that Dr. Becker had been evasive and uncooperative, and that consequently they would need many more days of cross-examination. Matias expressed sympathy for their complaint, which the lawyers took as a license to further criticize Dr. Becker. "I never bargained for all this," he said to me in disgust at the behavior of the lawyers, who continued to claim that their clients' constitutional right would be denied if they did not have an unlimited right to cross-examine Dr. Becker.

When we returned to the hospital we learned we had been ordered to meet on Wednesday morning with Stephen Landaw, the head of research at the hospital.

Wednesday Morning

We went to Landaw's office where he and his assistant, Bill Kelly, were waiting.

"Marguerite Hays called me," Landaw said to Dr. Becker.

"So?"

"Do you know her?" Landaw asked.

"I have spoken with her on the phone," Dr. Becker replied.

"She spent a week here four years ago," Kelly interjected, "for training in research administration when you were the head of research. She complained that your treatment of her was disrespectful because she was a woman."

"I don't remember that," Dr. Becker replied.

Landaw resumed speaking: "She said your present activities were not in the best interests of the VA and she didn't care about your reasons."

"Referring to what?" Dr. Becker asked.

Before Landaw could answer, Kelly interjected, "I have been collecting clippings of newspaper articles regarding your opinions about the safety of powerlines and sending them to her, as she ordered me to do." He opened a folder and spread some articles on the table. Landaw picked up the articles and began reading quotes attributed to Dr. Becker, which he could quickly locate because they had been underlined:

"'The official line in this country is that electromagnetic energy has no effect on biological systems. We believe that we have found that this is not true.' Did you say that?" Landaw asked.

"Yes," Dr. Becker replied.

"Did you also say: 'The predicate therefore exists for an inquiry into whether such effects will be caused by powerlines?'"

"Yes."

"You were quoted as saying: 'The problem is now one of continuing the research during a time when tight money and cutbacks haunt the academic community.' Did the reporter quote you correctly?"

"Definitely."

"How about this quote: 'At one time we could employ three research assistants; it was a good arrangement, we got more work done and they learned, but now the funds have dried up.' Did you say that?"

"I did."

"And the quote that particularly incensed Dr. Hays: 'The powerline should not be built until a comprehensive study is made of the impact it will have on the environment.' Did it misrepresent what you said?"

"Absolutely not," Dr. Becker replied, and then asked, "What exactly is her problem?"

"She said she is receiving inquiries from state and federal agencies about your campaign against power companies, and complaints from power companies and trade organizations regarding your use of the VA as a pulpit to criticize how they run their business. The VA research service has never received this level of attention," Landaw asserted.

"We can agree on that point," Dr. Becker responded.

"She recognized that you have done much fine work, and emphasized that you had been well rewarded with funds, personnel, laboratory space, recognition, and your appointment as a Medical Investigator, which afforded you the freedom to follow your scientific intuition. But she said that as long as she was the head of research at Central Office, no one in such a coveted position as a Medical Investigator would be permitted to make the research service an object of controversy. She said that the mission of the VA research service is to advance veterans' health, and that was not what your testimony was doing. So unless you change your ways immediately, she will take action."

"Meaning what?" Dr. Becker asked and Landaw answered, "You should immediately stop testifying and stop performing research related to powerlines or anything else that doesn't concern the health of veterans. Otherwise she will remove you from your position as a Medical Investigator. She said that was her decision, and that you should appreciate the wisdom behind it."

Dr. Becker responded: "She is happy if I publish papers as long as I don't do anything meaningful. But when my research has a direct application to human problems and I have the temerity to call attention to that application, then she quakes in her boots and orders me to return to the obscurity that makes her feel comfortable. She knows nothing whatever about research, and makes no effort to see that understanding the nature of chronic disease is the greatest service possible to the veteran because it is, by far, the greatest source of their misery. What she demands will never happen. I would never put up with that."

"She made it clear," Landaw said, "that she has nothing but contempt for your actions, whatever your reason. She repeatedly called you a stubborn man who set his personal agenda above the welfare of the VA, and said, 'As long as I am head of research, no maverick is going to be rewarded with a coveted job.'"

"She has previously spoken to me this way more than once," Dr. Becker said.

"And you still defy her?" Landaw asked.

Dr. Becker responded: "I do. She cannot intimidate me. All living things are closely tied to the levels of electromagnetic energy in the natural environment. Interactions occur by means of mechanisms and structures in the brain that are designed to perceive the normal changes in the earth's electromagnetic environment for the purpose of furnishing timing signals for biological cycles. The presence of abnormal man-made energy affects these mechanisms and structures, producing dangerous alterations in basic life functions, resulting in a wide spectrum of diseases. If you had uncovered all this in your research, would you keep silent?"

"She will follow through as she threatens," Landaw said. "She is the first woman to hold a position of power in Central Office, and I think she cannot allow you to defy her."

"She has forgotten what is important and cares only for her career," Dr. Becker replied.

"Maybe," Landaw said, "but you insult her and you are in her sights."

"The truth cannot be an insult."

"Your appointment as a Medical Investigator will end," Landaw said.

"I knew it wouldn't last forever. Now it will only end a little sooner than I expected. Could anyone embark on a course such as mine, surrounded by obstinate ignorance, and not expect severe hardships? Perhaps she does me a favor. Disemboweling my laboratory is of no importance compared with the pain I would have suffered had I not spoken out."

Landaw threw up his hands and shook his head, which prompted Dr. Becker to say, "You smile at me, Steve, and think me a fool, but the fool is the one who makes the threats against me."

Landaw didn't respond, so Dr. Becker asked, "Does she want anything more from me than my research job?"

"I think not," Landaw replied, and then turned to me and asked, "Andy, are you part of this plan?"

"Yes," I answered, but speaking sharply Dr. Becker said I had no right or duty to answer that way, and he told Landaw that I did only what I had been asked to do.

The lawyers for the power company had continued to argue that they needed more time to cross-examine Dr. Becker, and they threatened to ask that his entire testimony be stricken if their demand wasn't met. Simpson secured a promise from his agency that if Dr. Becker testified on two additional days, no further testimony from him would be required, and he agreed.

Thursday Testimony

The courtroom was heavy with tension when the hearing resumed. The lawyers were frustrated that they hadn't created a record that could undercut him. Before he took the stand I again asked him to avoid answering questions that went beyond what he had written about in his report.

Q. Doctor, during the past few days several of my colleagues have asked you about your opinions on human experimentation, but the record still remains unclear. Let me ask you; is it your impression that the proposed powerlines are being erected for any experimental purposes or research purposes?

A. That is not my impression.

Q. Doctor, could you tell me then what specifically it is about the proposal to construct the powerlines that falls within your definition of human experimentation?

A. Well, I would look at that in the following light. The only analogy I can draw is if instead of working with animals, we were to work with humans in our experiments. If I set up a human experimentation study involving the exposure of humans to powerline energy levels, that research would be subjected to human experimentation committee review, and we would have to then abide by all the pertinent regulations. If the establishment of the energy levels were not being done for the purposes of human experimentation, then I imagine it evolves into a legal question of whether or not you are experimenting on humans. The answer would depend on whether or not you knew that there was a question in regards to possible side effects, and whether or not you had any kind of a program to look for side effects.

Q. In other words, Doctor, the application of your philosophy with respect to human experimentation depends upon the purpose for which the proposed lines are constructed; is that correct?

A. No, I wouldn't say that. If you don't know what's going to happen to a human population when you do thus and so, and there is evidence that there may be harmful effects, would doing thus and so constitute human experimentation? In my own, and solely my own opinion, then I would say the answer is obviously yes. I don't have any opinion about the legal question because I am certainly not a lawyer.

Q. Doctor, in expressing that opinion, to what degree of certainty must you know the results of the application of a certain factor before the question passes out of the realm of experimentation under your definition?
A. And into what realm?

Q. The realm to which the human experimentation philosophy expressed would not apply.
A. That's a question I really can't answer. From a medical point of view, as a physician, if there were a possibility that something is harmful, then it would be beholden upon me to advise any patient that consulted me not to become involved unless they were fully apprised of the problems and did so of their own volition.

Q. Well, Doctor, under your definition of human experimentation, wouldn't your stipulation as to the required practices to be followed apply equally to the construction of a factor, for example, which might discharge some constituents into the air or water which may have presently unknown biological effects of which we were not certain?
A. It then evolves into a question of degree of certainty. If a factor is going to introduce a novel substance into the environment, I believe that it would be prudent to determine whether or not that substance would have any effect. If a factor is going to introduce a substance into the environment that has been shown to have some possible deleterious effects, and this discharge would involve a fair number of people, then I think that the same principles of human experimentation that I described would apply.

Q. Well, are you suggesting that these provisos be applied in the case of the powerlines?
A. Yes. In my opinion, if this was considered to be human experimentation, then certainly those rules should be applied.

Q. Doctor, would you agree that under your definition of human experimentation, the prescription of a drug by a doctor to a patient where he is unable to determine precisely whether or not there will be an adverse effect would constitute human experimentation?

A. Well, now, I think you are reaching a little far there. If you carried that to its ultimate, then any prescription constitutes human experimentation. The present interpretations of the ethical codes for the way we practice medicine hold that whenever a patient is advised to take a drug, or a drug is prescribed by a physician, that the patient should be apprised of the possible side effects of the medication. It also holds for surgical procedures and diagnostic procedures.

Q. However, Doctor, is it not true that the other rather stringent conditions applied to human experimentation with respect to establishing a committee, for example, risk/benefit analyses, are not generally thought to be applicable to a practicing physician administering drugs to his patient?

A. Well, to the extent that it does not require committee action before you prescribe a material, that is true. The risk/benefit and the voluntary considerations and the informed consent considerations all still hold. The risk/benefit is determined by the physician in his own mind, or it should be determined by the physician. Let us take a specific case in point. It might illustrate it better for you. If he is going to use one of the newer antibiotics, some of which have very definite risks involved in their usage, then the risk/benefit consideration is whether that antibiotic is the appropriate one to use for the infecting organism that the patient harbors.

If the physician makes this judgment and accepts a certain amount of risk in the prescribing of this medication, it is beholden upon him to inform the patient of the same risk.

Q. Do you believe that an activity which resulted in the discharge of a substance having a known adverse health effect into a populated area would necessarily constitute a practice classified as human experimentation by your definition?

A. It would be human experimentation if the total risk has not yet been evaluated. For example, say a factory is going to discharge something that is well known to be extremely hazardous, such as cyanide. Then there is no question as to whether or not ill effects will occur. If it is going to discharge a substance that has not been completely characterized as to all of its activities in respect of the human population but which is under considerable suspicion as being possibly productive of harmful effects, then the principles of voluntary participation in the experiment and the principles of informed consent then should be applied.

Q. Doctor, would you not agree that tobacco smoke, for example, could fall well within the substances you have just identified as having possible adverse effects?

A. You would find a large number of physicians who would agree with you. You would find some who would indicate that there still are some major discrepancies in the characterization that tobacco is a harmful substance. I am not absolutely convinced that tobacco is as harmful as some people tell us it is.

Q. Noting that you have been smoking a pipe for the entire proceeding, Doctor, would you characterize that as human experimentation with respect to the people in the hearing room?

A. Well, you raise an important point. Obviously, in respect to myself, no, because I voluntarily smoke the pipe. Secondly, I am well aware of all of the possible consequences that are supposed to occur as a result of it. In respect to the other people in the hearing room, I noted the court reporter also smokes, so I felt it not incumbent upon me to ask her if it was all right with her should I smoke a pipe.

Q. However, Doctor, you have probably noticed that I do not smoke. Have you asked me or have you asked anyone else in the room?

A. I did not ask you if you objected if I smoked. You raise a point which is being considered by the legislature, I believe at the present time, and in my opinion, it is a very valid point.

Q. Doctor, I am trying to get at what differentiates in your mind the necessity for going through procedures you have identified for human experimentation with respect to pipe-smoking, as opposed to the situation in which we are proposing, construction of a powerline? How would you reconcile those two apparent differences?

A. Well, my opposition to the proposed lines is based upon my opinion that they constitute basically an increase in the present levels to which the population may be exposed.

Q. Well, Doctor, prior to the time that you were a witness, I was not subjected to the same amount of pipe smoke as I am being subjected to today. How do you distinguish that particular fact in your analogy to the powerline?

A. I think again you're trying to compare apples and oranges. As I indicated before, I would be opposed to any technological developments that would result in an increased level of risk. Now, we're all exposed to a certain amount of tobacco smoke in the course of our everyday life. Attempts are being made now by the legislative authorities to limit this exposure and this I agree with and I'd be glad to live within the confines of those rules at that time.

Q. In view of my exposure, I hope you're right.

A. Well, in point of fact, it is very similar to some of the situations we have at hand, the crucial experiments have yet to be done.

Friday Testimony

Dr. Becker continued to prove a resilient witness, relatively immune to their design of attack. As the day wore on the lawyers became progressively more aggressive, but if anything he became more firm and resolute in his answers, the exact opposite of what they wanted, drawing strength, I thought, from the certain knowledge that his ordeal would end that day. His cross-examination ended just as I had seen so many of our conversations end, with him giving a short speech that succinctly described the situation and explained his point of view.

Q. Doctor, are you in favor of shutting down all powerlines because of the harm that might be caused by the electromagnetic energy they emit?

A. In response to the question whether I would recommend construction of the powerlines as they are now designed, I said "no" for the reasons that they are possibly productive of biological effects. And I go on to say that the most prudent course to follow would be to determine the complete spectrum of biological effects produced by exposure to the electromagnetic energy. This obviously includes existing high-voltage powerlines. As a scientist, I can only say that we think that we have positive evidence that effects of electromagnetic energy do occur in the biological organism. It seems to me quite within the realm of possibility that not only the existing powerlines but also the existing ambient electromagnetic energy from other sources, particularly in urban areas, is productive of biological effects at the present time. I would, however, not be in favor of turning off the electricity because of the other social factors that would appertain as a result of such an event. These would obviously be in the medical sphere as well as in the economic and social spheres. The possible medical value gained by turning off all of the electrical power at the present time would be counterbalanced by the medical harm that would be done as a result of disruptions in our entire society. So, I could not in good conscience at the present time say that I recommend the discontinuance of operation of all powerlines. But I do stand on my recommendations that a problem, in my opinion, does exist, that the problem will not go away and that it should be studied.

In the immediate aftermath of his testimony there was a lull in communications from Central Office, which he interpreted as part of the necessary preparations to fire him from his job as a Medical Investigator; he never doubted Hays would do that. Then at a laboratory meeting he read from a letter she had written him: "I regret to inform you that your position as a Medical Investigator has been terminated due to a scarcity of funds."

"What does that mean for the lab?" someone asked him.

"Nothing good," he answered. "I still have the basic grant that supports most of your salaries, but that could change. You should all think seriously about finding jobs elsewhere."

Dr. Becker operating the spectrophotofluorometer.

Dr. Becker and his wife Lillian the week prior to his testimony.

Marguerite Hays

Chapter 11.
Confrontation

1976–1977: He speaks to a national audience, is attacked by the president of the National Academy of Sciences, criticized by his neighbors, and loses all his funding for research

Regeneration remained the type of research Dr. Becker loved most but his circumstances required him to follow other paths. He continued studies of the effects of electromagnetic energy on animals, believing that line of research afforded him the best chance to expand the beachhead he had gained for his revolutionary concept of an analog electromagnetic regulatory system in the body. He also continued his acupuncture studies, becoming the most prolifically published investigator in that area, and was planning further experiments he hoped to begin after his NIH acupuncture grant was renewed.

In the powerline hearing the power companies presented Herman Schwan, Solomon Michaelson, and Morton Miller as expert witnesses. Simpson's agency required them to testify in Syracuse in return for my agreement to help him carry out their cross-examination, a process that lasted many weeks. Each evening I returned to the laboratory, but Dr. Becker had little interest in hearing about the details of what the three witnesses said so I told him only about their conclusions. Schwan said that the powerlines "will not be harmful or unsafe," Michaelson said that they produced "no demonstrable biological effect which may be hazardous to health or safety," and Miller said, "There will be no unreasonable risks to health or safety due to the powerlines." Their cross-examination yielded thousands of pages of testimony, the impact of which I summed up by telling Dr. Becker that they were thoroughly discredited and that Simpson thought nobody at his agency believed them, to which Dr. Becker responded, "That's appropriate."

But the experts' egregious errors in logic and biology were generally unappreciated in the popular press where the situation was typically styled as a dispute among scientists. This perception frustrated and angered Dr. Becker because it only helped the three experts succeed in duping the public. He had seen microwave ovens come onto the market even though their safety had never been demonstrated, followed by numerous other unvetted energy-emitting devices. He thought that most people would probably ignore any health risks these devices posed even if they knew about them; he also thought that was no license to avoid proper research or to disseminate misleading information about safety. From his perspective, neglect regarding proper research and education combined not only to trick people into causing their own diseases but also to thwart his life-long project of establishing the existence of an electromagnetic regulatory system in the body.

I saw presentations of the three experts in Washington, DC, at a conference organized by the Electric Power Research Institute and the Department of Energy to present results obtained by their research contractors, and I told Dr. Becker about what I had heard:

"Schwan talked about his calculations," I said, but before I could provide the details he motioned for me to move on and asked what Michaelson and Miller had said.

"They both think that new animal studies by Phillips showed powerline energy was safe," I said.

"That makes no sense," he replied. "The Sanguine studies, our studies, the work of many others, all say exactly the opposite. How did they get around that?"

"Phillips did many studies and repeatedly found no effects. Michaelson and Miller argued that the absence of effects was evidence of safety."

"Do you think they can get away with that?"

"I don't see what will stop them. Their position will probably sound plausible to a judge, especially if the court doesn't hear from you."

"Well it won't, not again."

I continued, "Their story is that if X number of studies that cost a few dollars report effects but Y studies that cost many dollars and are far more numerous say there are no effects, then there are no effects. The studies you listed are X, and their Y studies were manufactured by various contractors, Phillips being the most prominent."

"You think his studies are rigged?" he asked.

"I do," I said. "I think he designed his experiments to guarantee they wouldn't find effects." At that moment I had no understanding of the depth of the scientific misconduct Phillips had committed. I knew only what he had presented at the meeting and described in published reports, and had not yet gained access to documents that he never imagined I would see.

Dr. Becker didn't respond to what I had said so I spoke up and asked if he had ever come across investigators who rigged their studies so that the result would be what they wanted. He nodded as if to say "yes."

"We are in a vise. Perhaps you should consider changing your approach," I said.

"What do you mean?" he asked.

"You have done as much as you could to create awareness of the side-effects problem. But I don't think ordinary people can hear you, and there is nothing you can do about that. It might be better to return to the old days when we were not in the public spotlight, had more money for research, and aggravated fewer people."

"So you think we are just throwing ourselves on the tips of the enemy lances."

"Every time you produce evidence to support your view, they will produce evidence to the contrary, which is easy because anybody can find nothing, and which is more or less expected because there is nothing at all in the biology textbooks to suggest that you should find something."

"Sometimes bad science drives out good," he replied, "but your proposal that I should slink away is unacceptable. You can make your own choice. I will continue with the experiments, write the papers, and let the chips fall where they may. There is no other possible course."

He received a phone call from Senator Gaylord Nelson, who was the head of the subcommittee that controlled the funding for the Sanguine studies. Nelson asked Dr. Becker for his opinion about the safety of the antenna, and soon thereafter Nelson held a press conference during which he announced he had learned about a report of a committee of experts assembled by the Navy to evaluate the safety of Sanguine. He said, "It appears that the Navy kept the wraps on the existence of this report because it contains the very first scientific evidence that Sanguine indeed would have an adverse environmental impact. Up to this moment this was a matter of concern and conjecture. Now there is hard evidence that must be pursued." He quoted Dr. Becker's response to the question whether the antenna posed hazards to human health: "The Navy studies produced adequate evidence that the biological effect of a Sanguine-type system would be considerable." Then Nelson called for "an independent scientific review of the Navy's biomedical research connected with Sanguine, including classified research."

Dr. Becker respected the Navy for its efforts to understand the health-related implications of the antenna, and regarded its research as the kick-starter for the process of risk evaluation that he had advocated for so long. Absent the Navy's interest and financial support, he was certain that the work done at its research laboratories in Bethesda, Pensacola, and Johnsville, and the Navy-funded investigations performed at various universities, would never have been undertaken. Although he saw the Navy's goal as similar to his, his attitude about the Navy was complex and shifted as events unfolded. This was particularly so after he learned that the Navy had cancelled all its research contracts with the university investigators, terminated its in-house studies at the various Navy laboratories, and had withheld the committee report from the US Senate for more than two years. I believe those were the reasons he spoke so bluntly to Senator Nelson, although I may be wrong because he never explicitly said so. He had always been on good terms with high-ranking Navy officials, and recognized that any environmental health hazard posed by the antenna might be outweighed by considerations of national defense or other nonscientific factors. That point we did talk about. "If that's the case," he said, "they should say so."

A few days after the press conference Paul Tyler announced that he had asked Phillip Handler, the president of the National Academy of Sciences, to provide a re-evaluation of the Sanguine studies. Handler picked Schwan and Michaelson for the job and they quickly produced a report that, unsurprisingly, said the antenna would be completely safe. A strong public outcry occurred within days of Tyler's release of the report, and essentially every community in the Upper Peninsula went on record in opposition to the antenna. In response, the Navy contracted with Handler to appoint still another committee to evaluate the Sanguine studies.

***

For you to understand the events I am about to describe I must explain the significance of the Navy's contract with Handler and the National Academy of Sciences, and tell you something about the Academy and the man, who was like Dr. Becker in some ways but opposite in most ways two men could differ.

The National Academy of Sciences was only an honorific society until

1959 when Handler became its president. He was a biochemist, well known for his opinion that science was free of human emotions or values, and was therefore the supreme form of knowledge. He frequently expressed strong personal views regarding the important questions then occurring at the interface of science and society, championing nuclear power, a strong military posture, and the healing power of pharmaceuticals. He was hostile to environmental constraints, social programs, and the general drift of the times, which he said subverted the youth. He regarded his opinions as scientific facts in the sense that all properly educated and experienced scientists would have the same opinions if they evaluated the available data using the scientific method.

Under his leadership the Academy became a resource to which government agencies having a problem that sounded in science or stakeholders seeking slanted analyses of disputed scientific questions could turn for help. His views typically coincided with those who wanted his help and could pay for it. The historical fact was that no client of the Academy ever received a decision that was either unanticipated or contrary to Handler's personal opinion. These outcomes were guaranteed because of an enormous power he possessed, the absolute right to personally choose the members of all Academy committees. Committee members typically were prominent academic or industrial scientists, only a few of whom on each committee were experts in the problem under consideration; he rarely appointed members of the Academy. More than a thousand employees served at his pleasure and were available to manage the technical details involved in the deliberative process and in the wordsmithing of a final report. He controlled the work product of each committee like someone with a fish on a hook.

Critics of Academy committees frequently pointed to the biases of some committee members and the lack of balance among the knowledgeable committee members, complaining that the conclusions in the reports were foreordained. But such criticism almost always had no legs because of the public's great respect for the National Academy of Sciences, in whose penumbra the reports issued by Handler's committees were always seen.

After Handler died the power of the president of the National Academy of Sciences decreased greatly. Today it seems difficult to imagine that one man could have so thoroughly controlled the public narrative of science, but that was the case in 1976, which is the time I am now writing about. Handler was the czar of establishment science, and that was a bright fact of life for Dr. Becker as he made his decisions and plotted his course of action.

***

One morning Dr. Becker asked me to come to his office. With a grim countenance he said, "Handler announced his appointments to the Sanguine committee."

"What's the problem?" I asked.

"Schwan, Michaelson, and Miller are on the committee," he said angrily.

"Who else?"

"Nobody that matters, except Adey, who is a coward and will never speak up."

"Who is the chairman?"

"Woodland Hastings, the head of the biology department at Harvard."

"Do you know him?"

"I know of him, a biochemist. He works on bacteria."

"Are you going to contact him?"

"No. I'll write to Handler."

"Do you have any objection if I contact Hastings?"

"No, but I doubt anything good will come of it."

Looking back now, far less impaired by the fog of those days, I think Dr. Becker must have sensed that the progress he had made in advancing an integrationist perspective and in identifying a place in experimental biology for electromagnetic regulation of life were in mortal jeopardy because of the selfish motives of one powerful man. But at that moment he said very little to me concerning his deepest fears, if he had any. What I saw was resoluteness, which was unsurprising to me because in my mind it was the character trait that defined him.

Hastings and I spoke and corresponded during the next two months. After each contact I reported to Dr. Becker what I had learned, and he encouraged me to continue despite his low expectations. Initially Hastings was warm and receptive. He told me scientists from several universities in Michigan had spoken highly of Dr. Becker's research and of his testimony in the powerline hearing. Hastings said Handler had personally asked him to chair the committee and had overcome his reluctance by promising that the Academy staff would do all the necessary investigative work. I wasted no time in telling Hastings that the presence of Schwan, Michaelson, and Miller on the committee would corrupt its deliberations. They had already said under oath that powerline electromagnetic energy, which was vastly greater than that from the antenna, would be completely safe. "What do you expect their opinions will be regarding the antenna?" I said. I went further and told him about the details of their cross-examinations, things that I had actually seen—Schwan saying he reads only papers that failed to find effects because he knows any paper that finds an effect must be wrong; Michaelson saying that his experiments on cooking dogs in micro-wave ovens showed that levels that didn't cook were safe; Miller saying he took money to do research on the effects of electromagnetic energy even though he believed there were no effects because "He who has the gold makes the rules." Hastings told me he was "shocked" by this information, and that he had assumed everybody on the committee was an unbiased expert because "that was the way Dr. Handler worked." When I told him that none of the others on the committee knew anything about the subject with the sole exception of Adey, Hastings then promised me that if all that I had said were true, "then either Schwan, Michaelson, and Miller are off the committee and Becker is on it, or I'll resign."

During a subsequent conversation Hastings said he was "desperately" seeking Dr. Becker's appointment but that Handler seemed unwilling to change the committee makeup, something Hastings said Handler "had never done during the seventeen years he had been president of the National Academy of Sciences." In the end, Handler not only declined to appoint Dr. Becker, but, in an apparent attempt to offend him, Handler invited Dr. Becker to testify before the heavily biased committee.

Dr. Becker and I talked about how he intended to respond to Handler.

"Handler surely knows that only one point of view is represented on the committee, and that the safety issue won't be evaluated impartially," I said.

"Not the way the ordinary guy thinks the National of Academy of Sciences works," he replied, "but it is what it is."

"The committee's deliberations will be a charade. Even children can see it will conclude that the antenna has no public-health consequences," I said.

"It will probably do more than that," he commented. "Somewhere in their verbiage they will say 'no further research needed.'"

"Do you think we should send a letter to Handler?"

"Yes, as I told you earlier."

"It won't affect the committee's course and will surely aggravate Hays."

"I am aware of that," he said with a sardonic smile. "She keeps reminding me that I work for the Veterans Administration, not the Environmental Protection Agency or the Department of Health. But she is nothing more than a flunky."

"But a flunky with teeth," I said.

"True, unfortunately," he replied.

"Do you think that the letter will jeopardize the existence of our laboratory?"

"If we don't speak out, some form of the laboratory will probably survive as long as I practice medicine at the hospital. If we do, well, Hays has made it clear what she thinks."

He asked me to write a draft of a letter that said the composition of the committee was inimical to the pursuit of truth, that electromagnetic energy from the antenna may cause biological and ecological effects, that a great deal more research is needed, and that he recognized issues of national security might be involved. Then we began discussing Handler.

"He is a powerful man," I said.

Dr. Becker puffed on his pipe several times and then said: "He is weak because he has no ethical mooring and will do anything that furthers his outlook and generates funds, and because he lives in constant fear of open debate. Szent-Gyorgyi has been in the Academy for twenty years. He knows a lot about the biological role of electromagnetic energy but Handler didn't put him on the committee for fear of what he would say, just as he fears what I would say. Scientific truth emerges through consensus but consensus emerges through intellectual conflict, something Handler hates."

When I gave him the final draft he read it, slowly unscrewed the cap of the old-fashioned fountain pen he always used, and signed it.

In June an article in *Science* told the story behind the letter from the points of view of Hastings, the three experts, and Dr. Becker. Handler's name was not mentioned. The article said, "Hastings' committee had been hit with charges that it is 'rigged' and 'biased.'" Hastings was quoted as saying that some members of the committee "indignantly" denied the charges and effectively accused Dr. Becker of bias. The writer said some committee members believed there were "serious flaws" in the way the committee was formed, but Hastings said that the conflict of interest Dr. Becker described was "ridiculous." Hastings also said he had considered adding Dr. Becker to the committee, but that his letter had disqualified him. Schwan said that the letter "intimidates my freedom of expression," and Miller said it was "slanderous to my integrity." Dr. Becker said it was "inconceivable" that the three experts would conclude that the antenna was a potential health hazard "regardless of the evidence adduced."

About two weeks later Hays made a series of phone calls to the hospital director and the head of research at the hospital demanding that the local infrastructure support provided for our laboratory be systematically reduced to "below the critical threshold." The news was not intended for Dr. Becker's ears and came to him indirectly from several sources, one of which told him she acted out of anger and another that it was with pity.

He had previously faced existential threats and overcome them with the help of friends who worked in the hospital and at Central Office. Now he seemed to have fewer friends and more enemies. Nevertheless his opinions and research aims remained rock solid, as did his intention to do what he thought best no matter the cost. He told his congressman, James Hanley, about what Hays was doing and Hanley talked about it directly with Max Cleland, the administrator of the VA. Hanley told Dr. Becker that Cleland spoke highly of the regeneration research, expressed surprise that Dr. Becker's laboratory was under threat, and promised that no actions would be taken until he investigated the matter. Hanley also made it clear that Cleland was dealing with other matters, and that each decision he made was a political decision requiring him to consider the pluses and minuses with regard to the entire Veterans Administration.

While he was making his plans to continue his acupuncture research but before he could set those plans into motion he received a letter from the NIH cancelling his acupuncture grant. I asked him what reason had been given and he read from the letter, "Previous efforts have been unproductive." He contacted the chairman of the committee that had peer-reviewed his application for continued support and asked for an explanation, pointing out the only reason given was the opposite of the truth. The chairman told Dr. Becker that the committee had approved his proposal and recommended it be funded, so he was left to wonder why NIH administrators did not do so. "Obviously there is a reason," was all he said.

Richard Clark, a producer for the CBS television show "60 Minutes," contacted Dr. Becker regarding his letter to Handler's committee and the subsequent *Science* article, and Dr. Becker agreed to be interviewed by one of the show's reporters, Dan Rather, for a story about the Sanguine antenna. Clark and Rather came to the lab and their crew recorded Dr. Becker in some of his typical activities—treating a patient with the Becker Box, overseeing experimental surgery on a rabbit, and making an electroacupuncture measurement on a volunteer. Then he and Rather sat in the area of the laboratory where I normally worked and began talking off camera.

"You seem to have raised quite a ruckus, Dr. Becker," Rather said.

"Seems that way," he replied.

"It looks like everything began with that 1973 report by the committee you were on."

"That's when my involvement began."

"It minced no words regarding what the committee thought the Navy should do," Rather said, and reading from his notes he continued, "Under the heading 'Urgent and Absolutely Necessary,' the committee recommended further animal and human studies."

"Yes."

"Did that happen?"

"No."

"Why not?"

"You will have to ask the Navy."

"Do you think the Navy is trying to hide the truth about the health risks of the antenna?"

"I think their efforts to publicize it have been unnecessarily weak."

"Are you telling me there's a possibility that what comes out of the antenna could cause human disease?"

"Yes."

"Like heart disease or stroke?"

"Yes."

"You do know that's a mind-blowing thought for a lot of people?"

"I'm aware of that."

"Come on, Dr. Becker, the Navy says that a housewife is exposed to more electromagnetic energy in the course of doing her day-to-day chores than she would be from the Navy's antenna."

"How does the Navy know that the housewife is safe? We can't have it both ways. I and other physicians use very small amounts of electromagnetic energy to treat bone diseases. We apply that energy under very carefully controlled conditions. In my studies it's mostly done in the hospital and I see the patient every day. But it's a double-edged sword. If carefully controlled electromagnetic treatments can heal bones, why can't uncontrolled exposures from household appliances produce bad effects?"

"Do they?"

"We don't know. That's the point. We should look."

"At the energy from the antenna?"

"That's right," Dr. Becker said. "I was a member of the first committee to evaluate the biological studies that were performed for Project Sanguine. And I most certainly sat there and listened to several studies that had very definite effects. Animals that are exposed grow at a slower rate than control animals. A number of projects have shown this to be true. The second area in which definite effects do appear is that exposure to this type of field seems to produce stress. That possibility emerged from their human studies in Clam Lake and Pensacola."

"Won't all this come out when the NAS committee looks at the facts?"

"It's unlikely."

"Why?"

"Because the committee was pre-loaded with men who have already made up their minds."

"Dr. Becker, are you telling me that an NAS committee is rigged?"

"That's exactly what I'm saying."

"Are you willing to say that on the air?"

"Yes."

With the cameras running Rather asked Dr. Becker about the committee report Senator Nelson had publicized: "Is it true that the Navy repressed that report for better than two years?"

"The Navy did not disseminate the report widely," Dr. Becker replied.

When Rather asked about how the Navy dealt with positive reports its research had uncovered, Dr. Becker replied, "We know of, I believe it's five specific projects in which positive results were obtained, when the projects were terminated and the money just disappeared. There was no more to continue the work."

"Now, is this a definite pattern?" Rather inquired.

"It appears to be," Dr. Becker answered.

Rather spoke directly to the television audience and summarized what Dr. Becker had told him earlier about what the NAS committee had said: "Meanwhile, the Navy has called in the National Academy of Sciences to oversee and evaluate further experiments. And the NAS Committee has issued a one-sentence interim report saying that, so far, they think [Sanguine] is safe. But Dr. Becker isn't impressed. Some members of that NAS panel have previously testified publicly that radiation, similar to that of [Sanguine], isn't harmful. And Becker maintains it would be awkward for them to change their minds in public."

On camera, Dr. Becker expressed the sentiments that Rather had just summarized: "For example, if a person has already publicly gone on record that the Sanguine antenna is harmless, then obviously he cannot do an about-face and say the Sanguine antenna may be harmful. So that a number of people on this committee, I would feel, have a pre-bias."

"Is what you're trying to say that we're playing with a stacked deck?" Rather asked.

"I think so, yes," Dr. Becker replied.

Soon after the telecast of the interview, Phillip Handler wrote to the president of CBS, "I was shocked to hear Dan Rather suggest that a committee of the National Academy of Sciences is, in his words, 'a stacked deck.'" Handler protested, "The 'stacked deck' to which Mr. Rather referred is a committee appointed by me in response to a request from the US Navy." He said, "The notion that this committee is 'stacked' would be laughable were it not for the tragedy that the integrity of the committee and that of the academy were impugned so casually—or deliberately—by CBS News." He called the assertion that the committee was stacked "quite intolerable," and demanded an apology.

Handler also complained bitterly to Hays, saying that Dr. Becker was a "loose cannon," and that his papers claiming low levels of electromagnetic energy had caused stress in animals were not believable because they had been refuted by other studies. He wrote that "the leitmotif remains the same for Dr. Becker's other studies: a preponderance of the data showing no effects and some data purporting to indicate small effects of uncertain relation to the public health, all without a guiding theoretical background.

He predicted his committee would reject Dr. Becker's ideas and approve the antenna when it issued its final report, and his predictions came true. At a press conference in Washington, Hastings announced that the committee gave Sanguine "a clean bill of health."

Hays communicated with Dr. Becker indirectly through people in Central Office whom she controlled, and unknowingly through others who worked there and respected Dr. Becker but disrespected her. He learned that Handler had demanded that Hays fire him "for the good of the VA," but that she told him she lacked the power to do so. She did, however, have the power to close the laboratory, and she sent him a letter saying that all his Central Office VA research funds were terminated "effective as soon as practical under existing constraints and obligations."

A few days after he received the notice of termination of research support he came over to my desk, ostensibly to give me some guidance regarding how events might unfold, and how much time I had to make plans in the best interests of my career and my family. He told me that my salary was safe for at least a year, but that the work conditions would be quite different, there would be less space, and essentially no funds for supplies, equipment, or travel. He held out the possibility of funding for one additional year, pending the development of some contingency he didn't describe, but advised me not to factor that possibility into my plans. He told me he had accepted an offer to write a book about the electromagnetic growth-control system and wanted me to be a co-author. He suggested that I spend my time working on the book.

One of Dr. Becker's neighbors asked him about what she thought was an unusually high cancer incidence where they lived, an area south of Syracuse known as Sentinel Heights. He visited the locations where several people who had developed the disease lived and saw that their houses were very close to powerlines and had a direct line-of-sight to large antennas on the top of the hill. He learned that the powerlines transported low-frequency energy to two antenna farms on the hilltop, where the energy was converted to high frequencies by about fifteen television and communications antennas.

Dr. Becker had once worked with a physician in England named Stephen Perry who had observed what he thought was a relation between exposure to the electromagnetic energy from powerlines and the occurrence of depression that resulted in suicide. Dr. Becker sent Perry the equipment needed to measure the energy, which he did at the address of each suicide victim in his medical district and at an equal number of control addresses. They found that the energy levels were higher than normal at the addresses of the suicide victims, and their study was published. The report hadn't caused even a ripple of interest among public-health authorities, so he declined all subsequent requests to become involved with epidemiological studies. But the presence of two types of electromagnetic energy in association with cancer intrigued him, and he got the idea that the cancers might have been caused by the simultaneous action of the two kinds of energy during its path to and from the antennas, an idea that had never been tested or even proposed.

He made a topographical map showing the locations of the powerlines and antennas in relation to the address of every family that lived on the Heights, about four hundred addresses. From personal investigation he learned that there were seven cases of cancer during the preceding five years that had occurred at addresses on his map. Six of the cases had occurred at addresses exposed to both forms of energy, all located on the north side of the hill along a direct line-of-sight to the antennas. He found only one other case, at an address that was near powerlines but was shielded from antenna energy by a natural outcropping of the hill. When he compared the overall number of cancer case on the Heights to the number expected based on the known prevalence of cancer in the county, he saw that the frequency of cancer on the Heights was more than 50% greater than expected. All environmental factors known to be associated with cancer were absent on the Heights.

He had no doubt that publication of the results was justified because they introduced the novel possibility of a synergistic phenomenon involving electromagnetic energy from different kinds of sources. He ignored advice that the work was premature and inflammatory, and reported it in the *New York State Journal of Medicine*, concluding that the location of the cases in relation to sources of low-frequency and high-frequency electromagnetic energy was "suggestive of a relationship" sufficient to "justify appropriate epidemiological studies of this and similar sites throughout the State."

At about the same time, several Syracuse television stations purchased land on the Heights and asked the local zoning board for permission to erect new antennas. A controversy developed between residents on the Heights who favored and those who opposed granting the permission. Dr. Becker's report in the medical journal surfaced, and he was asked to give a talk about his findings at a public meeting to be held in the basement of a local church.

When he arrived to give his talk he saw people standing outside the church and asked why they hadn't entered. He was told, "They are probably waiting for their leaders." In a surprised tone he asked what organization the people belonged to and was told, "They don't have a name, it's informal, mostly people who disagree with what you are going to say." "How do they know what I'm going to say?" he asked. "I haven't said anything." Someone told him that the people had heard about his article in the medical journal and thought that it would lead to bad publicity and hurt property values. Dr. Becker asked whether the people had been given a copy of his article, and the gist of the reply was that it had been made available but that the language was too technical, which was why the meeting was organized.

Inside the church everyone was standing because there were no chairs. As more and more people entered the room, some pushing and shoving occurred between people who had differing opinions regarding what they thought Dr. Becker would say. No one made an effort to introduce him so when it became clear that no more people could fit into the room he began to speak where he stood, which was near one of the walls. Immediately after he identified himself the head of the zoning board spoke out, complaining that Dr. Becker shouldn't be leading the meeting. He replied that he had been asked to talk about his research and that was all he intended to do.

Someone called out that there were differences of opinion and that both sides should be able to speak. Dr. Becker said he had no objection and tried again to continue his talk but a man cut in, accusing Dr. Becker of trying to destroy the property values on Sentinel Heights. "He's doing it indirectly, but believe me that's what he's doing," the man said. Some people booed and others cheered.

Another man yelled that Dr. Becker's objective was to prove that the zoning board had blundered when it approved construction of the power-lines and antennas. Dr. Becker became visibly annoyed but quickly recovered and said, "I came here to talk about my study. If you don't want to hear what I have to say, I'll leave." Loud applause ensued from both those who wanted him to talk and those who wanted him to leave.

An engineer who worked for one of the television companies that had an antenna on the Heights called Dr. Becker a "so-called expert" and said, "He leaves the impression there probably are dangers. He doesn't really say it, but he leaves that impression. The truth is that people don't have to worry. They're worrying for nothing." Dr. Becker told him, "Just on a logical basis, you would have to say that somehow the powerlines and antennas are affecting us." Unmoved, the engineer responded, "There is no major problem." Dr. Becker replied, "Maybe not, but I think it's something worth investigating. Hopefully an appropriate agency will put some money into this, because no matter what city you go to, there will be places like Sentinel Heights."

Amid clapping from the crowd the engineer continued, "There are effects on certain cells, certain processes. But nothing says they are harmful. I've been around powerlines and antennas for thirty years. In all that time there has been nothing that has emerged in the way of a pattern of harm. If something is wrong, it surfaces. It always develops a pattern which is detected." When the engineer finished saying what he had to say, some people began arguing with one another in small groups. Dr. Becker looked around for a few moments, walked through the crowd, went up the steps, and left the church.

The next day we spoke only briefly about what had happened, but I remember vividly what he said, the last word he ever spoke to me about that meeting: "Ordinary people are no different than scientists, they believe what they want to believe." Then we began discussing the events that led to his loss of favor at Central Office.

"The evening in New York when Tyler asked me to serve on the Sanguine committee was the turning point in my career. It led to antagonism toward me in Central Office, something I never previously experienced."

"Do you have any regrets?" I asked.

"I'm confident I made the right decisions, and if I could do it all over again, I would make exactly the same choices."

"How do you account for the way Hays has treated you?"

"She is petrified of Handler. She knows the influence he can exert at Central Office, and she will avoid incurring his wrath at all costs. Her unnatural enmity toward me only makes her task easier."

"Handler is different from anyone I've ever known," I said, "power-hungry, dogmatic, pompous, with a close-minded view of biology."

"But he wasn't a spontaneous mutation," Dr. Becker said.

"What do you mean?"

"When he first appeared there was already an entrenched mentality that facilitated his ambition to become the sultan of science he is today."

"What mentality are you talking about?"

"Handler, like Jaffe and Hastings, is a biochemist. They know little about cells, even less about organs, and nothing at all about how a living organism works as a unitary whole. Worst of all, they think it is unscientific to even try to learn how that happens. When they were students they were taught to think only in terms of molecules, so they learned to see only the details, never the big picture, the defining limitation of the establishment. Science is only a game for them, with no ultimate purpose."

"You seem to be saying that everybody else is wrong and you are right."

"Not everybody, but even if that were true it wouldn't change anything. Determining what's there is a matter of looking, not voting. Doing science solely to collect stamps rather than solve problems is irresponsible and wrong."

"Hastings lied to me, to the *Science* writer, and at his press conference. Why do you think he acted as he did?" I asked.

"Because that's what Handler wanted him to do. Hastings' service on the committee was his fifteen minutes of fame, and he probably believed what Schwan and Michaelson told him. Everyone around him tells him that electromagnetic energy is completely safe, so it must be completely safe. Think about the Salem witch trials. Everyone says she's a witch, so she must be a witch, and anyone who disagrees is also a witch. The desire to be part of the establishment is as natural for him as breathing. I remember that Hastings sided with Pittendrigh against Frank Brown, so Hastings' attitude towards electromagnetic energy is no surprise."

Sentinel Heights, NY

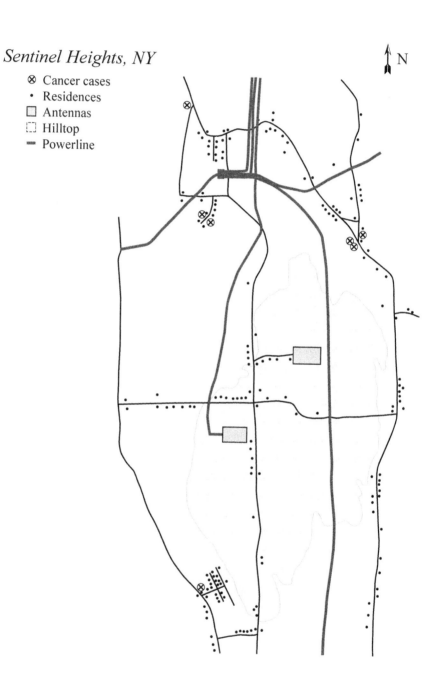

- ⊗ Cancer cases
- • Residences
- ☐ Antennas
- ⬚ Hilltop
- ▬ Powerline

N

The north side of Sentinel Heights in 1977

Phillip Handler

Chapter 12.
Exile

1978–1979: He seeks renewed funding, is deceived, contemplates the failure of scientific medicine, and goes into exile

Dr. Becker began working on his book about the electrical growth-control system, and I asked him how the idea originated in his mind and emerged from the scientific landscape.

"I was always fascinated by how living organisms worked. In medical school, during my first months on the wards when we made rounds our professor would emphasize the patients' signs and symptoms because they were what determined the treatment. But he would say almost nothing about the actual process of healing that took place in the patient. If the diagnosis and treatment were appropriate then healing was expected and the professor showed little interest in how it happened. Healing was obviously under precise control, and every part of the body seemed to know what the other parts were doing. Nevertheless healing was not regarded as a result of specific physiological laws, and there was nothing about them in the medical textbooks. I asked myself why it was that such widely different conditions as trauma, infection, cancer, and heart disease all triggered the same syndrome of healing, responses shared to such an extent that it was often impossible to determine what the original cause was by examining the patient during healing. Finding treatments for each disease was important, but not nearly so important as understanding the syndrome of healing that is superimposed on all diseases. The concept of healing remained with me and I decided to try to understand it."

"How did the idea of electromagnetic energy enter the picture?"

"I used the term in my early publications to refer to the factor responsible for the tissue changes that occur during healing. As the research developed I recognized that healing organisms always manifested a strong electrical change that occurred immediately at the injury site, followed by more gradual change and longer-lasting electrical signals that persisted throughout healing. It seemed obvious that the electrical factors could be controlling the ongoing biochemical changes. But the establishment regarded that thought as abominable. They still do."

"Why do you think the biologists are so antagonistic?"

"They don't believe something is possible if they can't explain it using their biochemical techniques. It's easier for them to resort to the techniques than to use their eyes and brain to make new observations and interpret novel observations made by others."

"So you think that the emphasis on techniques is misplaced?"

"Techniques are useful for solving known problems, but overemphasizing them suppresses intuition, which cannot be taught. Only a few have talent for really seeing what's there and finding problems. But those few phenomenologists are needed very much. Unfortunately the establishment regards them as less than true scientists because their work is partly based on instincts regarding the ways of nature."

"Will you write about this in your book?"

"I will describe the results I obtained and the reasoning that led to them. That's the most I can do to help those I want to help and defeat those whose make-up forces them to oppose any new ideas."

"They say that the exclusive basis of biology is biochemical machinery, but you say otherwise. I think you have a hard nut to crack."

"Electromagnetic energy is the true basis of biology, a reality that can be explored only by going beyond the orthodox mindset regarding how to do experiments. My intention is to show what can be observed if this idea is accepted, even if provisionally."

"What do you mean by that?"

"Living organisms must be allowed to behave according to their nature, not according to how someone pontificates that they should behave. They are dynamic and unitary, and can exhibit amazing behaviors in addition to the pedestrian behaviors that result from ordinary biochemical reactions of the type that can occur in test-tubes."

"Will you write about Galvani and Volta, and the controversy concerning whether the ghost in the machine was something physical or spiritual?"

"I must do so to set the stage for my discovery of the critical role of electromagnetic phenomena in the body. Only against the historical backdrop can one see the reasons for the delay until now in recognition of the true role of electromagnetic energy in biology. I am proposing that the ghost in the machine is physical but not biochemical, and I need to prepare the reader for this solution."

"You originated the concepts that the self-organizing and self-repairing phenomena of living things stem from their intrinsic electromagnetic properties such as semiconductivity and piezoelectricity. Are you going to emphasize the role of these and other solid-state characteristics of tissues?"

"Of course. Why would you even ask?"

"Those initial experiments were remarkable but further experiments that were needed to bring about general acceptance of the results weren't done. That lack of information would be a continuing obstacle to acceptance of your general theory if you were to base its validity on the results of your physics experiments. I think your theory would fare better if you emphasized the results of your biological studies."

"I have no reason to downplay my solid-state studies because none of them have ever been refuted."

"But the purpose of the book is to defend your large ideas. You can best achieve that goal by avoiding contentious issues and noncritical details, thereby reducing the number and venom of your critics. Except for the technology it spawned, physics has no serious place in the biology of electromagnetic energy. Shamos and Schwan were unimportant, but your plan would keep their errors alive. I say let them die. Your work in their area has served its purpose. There are more dangerous enemies that should be confronted in the book, I'm thinking of Weiss, Jaffe, Handler, and their kind."

"My observations have important implications for biology and medicine. I will describe my work to set the stage for an understanding of these implications. That is what I expect you to do as regards the other side of the coin."

"I don't understand what you are saying."

"The body's natural electromagnetic energy is the mechanism that animates the living organism, but by its nature that mechanism is vulnerable to abnormal electromagnetic energy produced by man and added to human living space. I will make the point that such energy endangers health and you will support the point by describing the biological effects in animals caused by electromagnetic energy from industrial sources. In this way, the underlying unity of both aspects of the role of electromagnetic energy will be revealed."

Unexpectedly, articles describing his regeneration research appeared in several popular magazines. He called the articles "nothing more than an irritation to the powers that be," but his attitude changed after a lobbyist named Don Yarborough visited our laboratory. He identified himself as an advocate for research that would benefit veterans with severed spinal cords, and he asked Dr. Becker about his work and its clinical implications.

"The salamander can regrow arms, legs, heart, brain, portions of the spinal cord and eye, as well as various internal organs," Dr. Becker told him.

"Do you think human beings could do the same thing?" Yarborough asked.

"Why not? Those structures are all anatomically similar to and as complicated as those in people."

"Then why don't severed spinal cords just heal?"

"I was studying that question when the establishment took away my grant support, so I have no firm answers, only some initial results," he answered.

"What results?"

"I found that regeneration was accompanied by certain electrical currents and voltages not found during less competent types of healing such as scar formation. These electrical phenomena appear to arise from the operation of a previously unrecognized system in the body that controls and regulates all forms of healing."

"You discovered this control system?" Yarborough asked.

"Yes," Dr. Becker replied.

"How does it work?"

"By means of very small electrical currents and voltages."

"Is that true?"

"I think so. If I'm right, then one could restore regeneration in higher animals by artificially producing the appropriate electrical environment."

"In your experiments have you done that?"

"In rats, which are normally not capable of regeneration, I regrew complicated portions of the foreleg with simple electrical devices. In man, using the same technique, I was able to stimulate healing of fractures that failed to heal. I believe regeneration of spinal cords in man would be possible with the proper electrical stimulation."

"This is the first time I ever heard a scientist say that the problem wasn't hopeless, that it is amenable to solution through research. This strengthens the hope of paraplegics." Then he paused and asked, "What research are you planning?"

"None," Dr. Becker replied. "My laboratory is being closed."

Yarborough said he had connections with the VA and Congress, and he offered to help arrange for the necessary funds. After he departed I asked Dr. Becker: "Do you think he could help us?"

"I don't believe in miracles," he replied. "The establishment controls all funding and regards my kind of thinking as too dangerous. It will block him."

The Paraplegia Cure Research Foundation, Yarborough's organization, asked Dr. Becker to be the lead speaker at a conference in Bermuda on multidisciplinary approaches to regeneration.

"Will you accept?" I asked.

"What would be the purpose?" he asked rhetorically. "They cannot help me or themselves. They have no understanding of their true enemy."

"Who is their true enemy?"

"The elites in the biochemistry departments of the universities. They exercise the prerogatives of high priests over the funding agencies. All biomedical science is under their self-serving yoke. They restrict the search for knowledge and prevent discovery of new ideas, so the search for understanding becomes more and more repetitious, mostly benefiting only the professors themselves."

"How do they benefit from that system?" I asked.

"Their advancement in position and prestige depends on the amount of research they do, not on its usefulness. Their kind of research can be manufactured in unlimited amounts in perpetuity only if it is trivial and noncontroversial."

I asked him whether he truly believed that regeneration of spinal cords was possible. At first he deflected the question, telling me that such research was not fated to be part of his future, but I persisted and he finally answered:

"We now know that regenerative growth is part of the total spectrum of reaction to injury, that it is related to specific electrical phenomena in the nervous system, and that it is amenable to analysis by system theory. I attribute the gradual diminution in regenerative ability as one ascends the phylogenetic scale to an increasing sequestration of the total neurological mass in the brain, with correspondingly less and less in the remainder of the body. I believe we can overcome this by supplying the electrical signal that the critical neural mass would supply, thereby creating an electrical environment which would support and encourage the cellular processes necessary for regeneration."

"Do you have a testable theory for why spinal-cord regeneration occurs in salamanders and not in people?"

"I call your attention to the phenomenon of spinal shock. I measured the electrical events that occur when the cord is cut and found that during the initial post-injury period the normal electrical measurements from the peripheral nerves that enter the cord below the level of the transection are abolished. In animals capable of cord regeneration, this phenomenon, called 'spinal shock' occurs only briefly. But in rats it is very long-lasting. I think this abnormally long period of spinal shock prevents occurrence of the cellular processes necessary for cord regeneration. Perhaps these processes could be stimulated by restoring the electrical environment."

His thinking about the potential importance of the Bermuda conference changed after he received a letter from Congressman Hanley who related what was said at a meeting he had with the VA's administrator, Max Cleland, and John Chase, its chief medical director. Hanley wrote that Cleland and Chase had "expressed a special interest" in Dr. Becker's regeneration research, which suggested to Dr. Becker that Yarborough might actually have the attention of the VA's highest officials. Dr. Becker accepted the invitation to speak at the conference and prepared a talk along the lines he had described to me, concluding that for those reasons he truly believed regeneration of spinal cords was possible.

When he returned from Bermuda I asked about the conference.

"It was terrible," he replied. "I gave my talk but it was a waste of time. Most of the others were biochemists and they had almost no interest in anything that was clinically relevant." But he smiled as he spoke and even before I could ask for an explanation he continued:

"Someone from the staff of Senator Allan Cranston was at the conference and he invited Yarborough and me to meet with the Senator in Washington during our trip home."

"You actually met with Cranston?"

"I did. He knew a lot about my work and said he had discussions with Cleland and other senators as well as with leaders outside government who were in a special position to pursue some of my suggestions. He told me that he wanted the VA to make clinically oriented spinal-cord research a priority, and that Cleland had agreed."

"What did you say?"

"That I thought it was impossible because Hays had turned the VA research program into a mini-NIH focused only on meaningless basic research, and that all the funding decisions were being made by her so-called peer-review panels, which were manned exclusively by establishment figures. In their eyes innovation is viewed as a bad thing. I have no place in such a system."

"What was Cranston's response?"

"That Rosalyn Yalow, who worked at the VA all her life and won a Nobel Prize, had said much the same thing. I told him I had just learned that I been nominated for a Nobel Prize, but that I thought neither the congress nor a Nobel Prize were powerful enough to change the system. Hays is four bureaucratic levels down from Cleland, but it's the bureaucracy not the administrator that runs the research program. Cranston said he understood that the research people in Central Office would have no political cover if they funded innovative programs that might not be recognized by peer-review groups."

"Where did that leave the issue?"

"Who knows? But Cranston told me that he was optimistic about the possibilities of positive action."

Several weeks after Dr. Becker returned from Bermuda, Hays notified him that her boss, Thomas Newcomb, the assistant chief medical director, had asked her to convene a meeting in Washington with Dr. Becker and others to acquaint Central Office officials with the state of the art in regeneration. She told Dr. Becker to prepare a formal presentation. I asked who would be at the meeting and he told me she wouldn't say but that he guessed they would mostly be people who believed that research is starting with something known and trying to understand its mechanism.

"You mean biochemists?"

"I mean people who reduce living matter to biochemistry. They now call themselves 'molecular biologists' in the hope, I suppose, that the renaming would imply it was something new. But it is still just biochemistry, a level of organization of living organisms so deep that even the idea of life has no meaning. Molecular biologists can synthesize genes and proteins, but they are not biologists any more than a typist is a poet or a paint-maker is an artist."

"Then you are saying that they have no possibility of bringing about regeneration as long as they restrict themselves to that level?" I asked.

"No seminal problem in experimental biology and no problem of interest in clinical medicine can be solved at that level. Thinking only in terms of biochemistry, it would have been impossible to discover that electromagnetic energy regulates limb regeneration, that it triggers cell dedifferentiation, that it makes bone heal, that it is a natural environmental cue for animals, or that it causes human diseases."

"So you anticipate the reductionists will be your antagonists at the meeting?"

"It's inevitable—virtually all those who make their living doing biological research are reductionists."

"So they can't deliver what Yarborough and Cranston and Cleland say they want, and yet you expect Hays will invite only people who favor that approach?"

"Not exactly. She is a clever witch. I expect there will be a few others who agree with me that an integrationist approach is essential to solve the problem. At the end of the day she needs to persuade Newcomb, Chase, and Cleland that she is acting on the basis of sound science after having fairly considered all points of view, so she must create the appearance of having done so."

When I saw him the day after the meeting at Central Office, he was infuriated. He told me Hays had invited five representatives from NIH and five biochemistry professors, and that they collectively criticized him "without reason or mercy," saying that spinal-cord regeneration was impossible, but that if the VA were willing to put up the money, they would do their best to try to grow new limbs, and that the attempt would begin with basic biochemical studies. At the end of the meeting, he said, Hays summarized what she perceived to be the pluses and minuses of the discussions. After he finished talking to me he went into his office and wrote to Newcomb.

> I found Dr. Hays' closing remarks incredible, and I trust that they do not represent a pre-conceived official position. Her message was that my work and that of my colleagues (both within and without the VA) is trivial, erroneous, or fabricated and obviously lacking in significance. The fact that this meeting was convened indicates that in some minds at

least, my concepts are significant and worthy of serious consideration. I realize that all of my research has been controversial. Nevertheless I believe that my record as a scientist during the past 20 years has reflected credit upon the Veterans Administration. Needless to say, it is discouraging to note that the administrative staff of my own organization still prefers to blindly adhere to dogma rather than be receptive to new ideas and evidence.

About a month later, in a Notice to all VA hospitals, Newcomb announced that tissue regeneration would henceforth be a "special emphasis area," and that research proposals in the area were encouraged. Dr. Becker announced his intention to apply for the funds and asked Hays what rules he should follow in writing his proposal. She told him that in recognition of his status as a senior investigator, his proven record of productivity, and his long history of being funded in the VA's research program for many years, a complex and detailed plan was unnecessary. It would be sufficient, she said, to describe his objectives and methods in general terms, paralleling what he had said during the meeting in Washington, and he did as she directed.

Several months later Hays notified him of her decision:

This is a very poorly written, overly ambitious, incompletely detailed research proposal. The review of the current status of work, background, and work accomplished varies from woefully inadequate to non-existent. The methods and procedures for all of the twelve objectives listed are given in one brief paragraph. Nowhere is it stated what data is expected from any of the projects, or how the resultant data is to be collected and analyzed. In short, it is impossible to draw any conclusions from reviewing the proposed research as to whether the stated objectives can be realized using the methods and procedures described. This is a very weak proposal that should be disapproved.

He protested that she had intentionally deceived him but she responded only to Yarborough and Cranston, who had mirrored the substance of his protest in letters they sent to her superiors. She told them and her superiors that the experts she had consulted were critical of Dr. Becker's research plan and that she would not reverse her decision because all research projects funded by the VA needed to be based on good science, not on "special pleading by complainers." She was his ally and supporter, she wrote, and did what she could to help him, but he was his own worst enemy. In comments to Yarborough she said her attitude was consistent and reasonable, and that Dr. Becker received the decision he deserved because he had been disrespectful to those who knew far more than he about regeneration. Her resistance against his indignant and repeated protests was necessary to oppose his ideas and prevent him from committing what she called the "crime of tampering with the peer-review process." She said the system worked the way it is supposed to work when evaluating proposals from an investigator who has a godlike confidence in his ideas and proposals, and a corresponding disrespect for generally accepted ideas. There was much anger in Dr. Becker's voice when he told me these things.

A short time later he came to the part of the laboratory where I worked and began to talk about how his life-long project had taken him to the place he then found himself in.

"Hays is like the three-headed dog that guarded the gates of Hades. One of her heads attacked me, another tricked the politicians, and the third licked the feet of the establishment. I can hear Jaffe and Handler laughing at what she has done to me."

"I suppose they are even more corrupt than her," I said.

"From the beginning of scientific biology people like them have happened, over and over. They are symptoms of the disease, harsh reminders that the underlying problem is the stifling power of the establishment."

"I have seen you encounter others like them," I said.

"Some were friends who became enemies. Some were colleagues who said or did whatever served the interests of their bosses. Some were strangers who if they could speak honestly would say they did what they did to feed their families. Some were devout believers in the establishment, like religious fanatics. Some simply did not have the brains that God gave a goose."

"Perhaps you could explain what Hays has done and try to convince people by choosing your words more carefully."

"The establishment will never change because of anything I say, even if I thought that trying to convince them with words was the right thing to do, which I don't. Convincing is for lawyers and politicians. Evidence is what scientists are supposed to use."

"Convincing words together with new and focused experimental results in appropriate proportions might succeed," I suggested.

"The problem is far deeper than you imagine. Experimental biology was founded on the myth that living organisms are collections of biochemical machines, like toothed gears in bags that mysteriously come to life when shaken. This myth is claimed capable of explaining all life, from the humblest earthworm to human beings, and therefore no new ideas are needed. For those who teach or believe the myth no amount of convincing would be enough, regardless of the evidence I produce."

"They say their research produces knowledge that someday will sum up to answer all the questions. You say that's impossible, and I believe you are right."

"Their research yields only the kind of knowledge that serves their interests, more grants and more publications, which are necessary for advancement in position and prestige. But this work has no necessary relation to human problems. Occasionally a useful drug is discovered, but never one that doesn't also cause harm because every gear in the bag is connected to every other gear."

"You are saying that the establishment concentrates on research involving biochemical technology, work that necessarily conforms to the founding myth but is devoid of innovation," I observed.

"They hate innovation. They much prefer a world where a later model of a machine is the only new thing that can happen. In the course of time they identify and solve simple problems, but the important tasks are officially declared to be unconquerable and are ignored. The only novelty they display is much more of a threat to man than a help to medicine."

"What do you mean?"

"The biochemists are playing God, tampering with portions of the living clockwork even though they have a totally inadequate base of knowledge concerning the whole clock. They conduct horrifying experiments on recombinant DNA, producing living chimeras that could possess new and deadly properties for the whole human race. The excuses for this Faustian behavior are that these experiments will, in some unspecified way, reveal to us useful facts about life. But the actual motivation is to profit from the new technology."

"The system you describe deserves contempt," I said.

"I could never fit into it because I would never accept the principle of blind adherence to an orthodoxy that cannot be questioned. I despise that idea and the experimentalists who propound it. They can live that way, I can't."

"Had I understood these things when I first met you I do not think I would have had the courage to accept your offer to work here, which would have been the worst mistake of my life."

The next time we spoke at length was in the den of his home on Sentinel Heights. Hunting rifles hung on the paneled walls along with many of his paintings, including one marked "First Prize."

"Where did you win that?" I asked.

"In the Adirondacks," he replied. "Lil and I bought land there. It's a beautiful place, a forest and trout streams, pastures that have reverted to the wild, and old barns. We built a log cabin with wood stoves and solar heating, and we go up there whenever we can." After pausing to fill and light his pipe, he took several puffs and continued: "We are planning to sell this house and move there."

"Is there no solution to our present problem other than for you to cease doing research?" I asked.

"I can no longer co-exist with the entrenched and self-defeating attitude of the establishment."

"What attitude do you have in mind?"

"A living organism is an integrated whole, all parts of which work together to produce something more than the sum of the parts. When the organism dies the parts are still there and many continue to function. What has gone is the communication and control system that negated entropy and imposed order and unification, and made possible memory, integrative thinking, growth, healing, sleep, pain, and life itself. How these phenomena come about is completely ignored by the establishment, which instead applies the ever-advancing technology of the inorganic world to a totally inadequate base of understanding of the organic, thereby collecting details about life rather than studying life itself. Their narrative of reality is fundamentally erroneous but irreversibly entrenched, championed by the academicians and the governmental agencies that fund biological research. Working together they determine the proposals that get funded, the manuscripts that get published, and the scientific opinions that get presented to the public regarding what constitutes scientific truth. The power of this gigantic governing structure power is far beyond anything I can overcome. My best course of action is to cease trying."

"Is the blindness of the establishment a good reason to stop practicing medicine?" I asked.

"Biologists followed the reductionist approach of the physical sciences and adopted the view that man was a simple machine. When they saw that the question of what life was could not be answered within their scheme they declared the issue to be a non-question, like asking what the soul was. That development had the devastating effect of preventing medicine from becoming modern and scientific, a development that is impossible under a system of thought that cannot identify the physical difference between something that is alive and something that isn't. The errors the establishment made deflected attention away from a scientific consideration of what life was and fostered the metaphor that human disease was simply the manifestation of a malfunctioning gear, the remedy for which was to oil it with a drug or replace it with a man-made part that, we are told, may even be better than the original. I recognize that the establishment's vision facilitated conquering the infectious and contagious diseases, but these quick-killing diseases were replaced by the degenerative diseases such as cancer, heart disease, and arthritis which maim or kill slowly and which increase constantly in prevalence, incidence, and severity. Medicine has no answers and can offer only the application and re-application of biochemistry and simplistic mechanistic procedures. The search for fundamental understanding and control of human disease has made little progress despite expenditures of enormous sums on research, almost all of it devoted to the study of the details of human pathology and almost none of it spent to uncover the actual causes of the diseases. The result of the establishment's seduction of medicine is that it has ceased being an empirical art and is now taught and practiced under the illusion that it is a precise technology. Physicians have become mere technicians who treat the machine but neglect the human being. The physician is no longer regarded as a guardian of life, but as the purveyor of mechanical services and is treated as such. Our treatment methods are increasingly costly in terms of dollars and quality-of-life of the recipients, and often produce side-effects that are worse than the original disease. The effort to create so-called scientific medicine that the establishment promised has failed, and clinical medicine has become a trade with no inherent moral character. I cannot accept this situation and cannot change it, so I must go."

"You are too young to go into exile. Won't you stay and try to change the situation, which you seem to understand so well?"

"We need to reject the mechanistic concept of life as based upon an inadequate foundation of basic knowledge. We need to study man and his functions and capabilities in the light of the functions and capabilities of all other life forms. We need to understand normal growth before attempting to understand abnormal growth. We need to re-purpose biomedical research so that it addresses the basic questions in ways that will lead to better understanding of life and its hazards. We need to revise the peer-review system so that it reflects true scientific judgment and is not a vehicle for suppression of new ideas. But there is no hope that these needs can be satisfied because the values they embody have been rejected. All that is left to the physician researcher who adheres to the idea of a scientific biology purposed to address man's problems is to renounce his desire to do research and his desire to practice medicine because he cannot accept its transformation from an art to a technical craft, like building boats. The issue is not whether I stay or go, I must go. But my mood is the same as it has always been, hating what the research establishment has done to medicine. I have no regrets except that I failed."

Epilogue

A superb researcher and clinician departed the day in 1980 when Dr. Robert O. Becker went to live the Adirondacks, where he remained in exile until his death thirty years later. He was succeeded by researchers who replaced stubbornness with compromise, defiance with acceptance, and action with argument. The best the world offers now is the bland and tepid research of the government and the establishment. The worst is the ruthless and cynical ambition of commercial and military interests. His selfless self-assertion has not been seen again.

In 1980 Marguerite Hays was sent from Central Office to a remote VA hospital where she worked as a radiologist for the next forty years and wrote a history of the VA research program extolling the progress it made under her leadership. In 1980 Lionel Jaffe was ordered by the president of Purdue University to apologize in writing to Dr. Becker for issuing a press release in which he called Dr. Becker's work "plain ordinary fraud," and he ultimately lost his faculty position. In 1980 Philip Handler was diagnosed with terminal cancer, and he died the following year.

Index

CPSIA information can be obtained
at www.ICGtesting.com
Printed in the USA
BVOW09s1534070218
507479BV00002B/227/P